Preface

The present book is similar in aim and design to its companion volume *Discovering the Greeks*. Its history is slightly different, but it has, like its predecessor, evolved from materials which have been used and tested in the classroom, carefully revised in the light of that experience. The age-range for which the book is intended is another similarity with our previous book, although we do feel that the present volume will have a greater appeal to middle schools and the upper forms of primary schools.

The reasoning behind the production of this book is that a knowledge of Greek Mythology is necessary for a full understanding of the Greek people and their earliest thoughts concerning their lives, their environment, the nature of the world, the elements and the universe; and likewise that this study of Greek Mythology, and the knowledge acquired from it, is indispensable for a proper understanding of Western culture, and especially its literature and art. And so, the objective of the book is to impart this knowledge. We feel that mythology is an ideal subject to form part of a Classical Studies Course in the early years of the comprehensive school, because of the innate appeal of the stories and their suitability for creative follow-up work. Therefore this book is designed to include, in a fixed and rational order, most of the better known myths and stories of legendary creatures. It is assumed (and advised) that great use will be made of visual stimuli, such as film, film-strip, illustrations from vase-paintings, to augment the copious illustrative material included in the book itself.

Once again, we are confident that teachers will welcome the work sections. They are designed to ensure that students have grasped the basic information in each section and, at the same time, to provide a launching pad for students and teachers to a whole range of creative and artistic activities.

Finally, we would express our thanks to all who in any way have helped with the production of this book.

Contents

Preface   iii

Part I GODS AND GODDESSES   1

  1 How the World was Made   2
  2 Cronos Rules . . . Zeus Takes Over   6
  3 The Gods of Olympus   9
  4 The Other Gods and Goddesses   16
  5 Kidnap!   18
  6 The Pain of Love   21
  7 Man is Created   25
  8 Prayer and Sacrifice   28
       Festivals for the gods   28
       Temples   31
       Sacrifices   32
       Tinker, tailor . . .   34
  9 The Great Flood   38
 10 The Dead   41
       Funeral customs   41
       Land of the dead   42
       Crime and punishment   45
 11 Orpheus and Eurydice   52

Part II STRANGER THAN FICTION?   56

  1 Crete: The Architect of the Labyrinth   57
  2 Crete: The Monster of the Labyrinth   60
  3 Crete: True or False?   64
  4 Troy: To War for a Woman   68
  5 Troy: Achilles and Hector   73
  6 Troy: The Death of a City   78
  7 Troy: Schliemann's Dream   82

Part III TRAVELLERS' TALES   86

  1 A Warrior Returns   87
  2 In Search of the Golden Fleece   93
  3 Mission Impossible   102
  4 A Strong Man Triumphs   108

Part I
Gods and Goddesses

1 How the World was Made

The Greeks had many stories about the world they lived in, about the things they saw around them every day, about gods and goddesses, about the great heroes of the past, about strange and wonderful creatures. These stories, some true, some partly true, some just imagination, are called Myths or Legends. We in Britain have our own legends—like the stories of King Arthur, of Robin Hood, of St George and the dragon. But we also enjoy hearing about the legends of the early Greeks. Most of these legends have survived to this day. In this book we are

St George and the Dragon

2

going to look at some of these myths. The first one tells us how (according to the Greeks) the world was made.

Since the beginning of time men have wondered how the world was made. You probably know the Bible story where we read that God made the earth and everything on it in six days, and on the seventh day he rested.

Maybe you have also heard of some scientists today who say that perhaps, billions of years ago, a huge mass exploded, sending out fragments all over space. Gradually these fragments, as they slowed down on their journey through space, cooled and formed stars, like the sun, and planets, like the earth. The scientists call this explanation the 'Big Bang' theory. Later, on the planet Earth, chemicals began to work together and gradually, over a very long period of time, different forms of life developed. From these, over millions of years, there evolved many different types of creature, including Man.

The Greeks had their own story to explain the beginning of the world. This story tells of the early gods and goddesses and their quarrels with one another.

In the beginning there was nothing but Chaos—a dark, shapeless mass where everything was hidden. Gradually, from this mass, came the goddess Ge (The Earth). She then gave birth to Uranus (the Starry Heaven) and Pontus (the Sea). From these three all the other gods and goddesses were descended. The earliest members of this divine family were the children of Ge and Uranus—twelve giants called Titans, including Cronos and Rhea (the mother of the later gods)— some horrible one-eyed giants called Cyclopes, and some ugly giants, each with a hundred hands.

Swirling gases in the galaxy—the beginning?

Cyclops, the one-eyed giant

3

Uranus

Uranus, however, hated his children—they were so ugly—and so he kept them hidden away under the ground. Ge, the mother, was angry and called upon her children to attack their cruel father and overthrow him. Only Cronos had the courage to do anything. He took a sickle and lay in wait. When night came and the huge Uranus returned and lay upon the earth, Cronos attacked him and cut off parts of his body. He threw these parts into the sea and from the bloody foam a new goddess—Aphrodite, Goddess of Love—was born. Cronos then released his brothers and sisters, and married Rhea. He now ruled over the Titans. Uranus was removed forever from the Earth.

A giant bone—what could it be?

Things to do

Section A

Put the heading *How the World Was Made*. Underline. Now answer these two questions:

1 According to the Bible, how were the world and all the creatures on it made?

2 How do some scientists say the world was made?

Now write down the sub-heading *The Greek Story of Creation*. Underline. Now try these questions.

3 Copy out these sentences filling in the blanks:

In the beginning there was nothing but . . . .

Gradually from this came . . . .

4

She gave birth to . . . .
It was from these three that all . . . .
Ge and Uranus had children who were . . . . ,
. . . . , and . . . .
4 Why did Cronos attack his father?
5 How did he attack him?
6 After the attack who now ruled the Titans?

Section B

1 Choose any scene from the Greek story of creation and draw
  a picture of it. Colour your picture and give it a title.
2 Find out the meanings of the English words 'chaotic' and
  'titanic'. How are they related to the Greek myth?
3 Millions of years ago, giants did in fact 'rule' the Earth.
  What were they? Draw a picture of one in your jotter and
  find out as much as you can about them.

2 Cronos Rules... Zeus Takes Over

Cronos was now ruler of the world and he immediately did what his mother had asked: he brought back his brothers from their prison beneath the earth where their father had kept them locked away.

Cronos soon began to worry and became afraid of his own children. He had been told that one day he would be attacked and overthrown by his own son, just as he had attacked his father Uranus. He was so scared that he decided to take drastic action. He swallowed his children alive, one by one, as they were born—Hestia, Demeter, Hera, Hades, Poseidon. His wife Rhea objected—Cronos did not listen; but soon after the birth of her youngest son called Zeus, she managed to trick Cronos. She wrapped a stone in baby clothes and Cronos swallowed that instead.

Cronos swallowing one of his children

Rhea presenting a stone in the form of a baby to Cronos

Meanwhile Zeus was sent away to the island of Crete and was there brought up in a cave hidden away below the forests of Mount Aegeum. He was fed on goat's milk and honey. A group of young men, the Curetes, made a loud noise every time the baby cried so that his father would never hear him or try to kill him.

Goats in the mountains of Crete

The cave of Dicte, on Mt Aegeum, where Zeus was hidden away

Cronos being sick

Zeus thus grew up safely, hidden away from his dangerous father. Soon he was strong and powerful. Rhea, his mother, had never forgiven Cronos for swallowing all her children, and so she was eager to help her son overthrow Cronos. She gave him a drink of mustard and salt. This made Cronos sick and he brought up first the stone and then all the children he had swallowed—Hestia, Demeter, Hera, Hades and Poseidon.

Zeus seized his opportunity. He declared himself to be the chief god of the world and of all the heavens. He allowed his brothers to draw lots for which parts they should rule. Hades won control of the land beneath the earth, Poseidon became ruler of the sea.

Zeus and his brothers then prepared to fight Cronos and the other Titans so that they could defeat them once and for all.

Zeus was helped in the fierce battle by the giants with one hundred hands whom Cronos had not released. Each hurling

Zeus releases the giants with the hundred hands

a hundred rocks at once, they easily defeated the Titans. The Titans were then banished to the Underworld, the Land beneath the Earth, where they were held as prisoners. Zeus now reigned supreme. He went to live on Mount Olympus and it became the home of all the gods.

Things to do

Section A

1 Write the heading *Cronos Rules*. Underline. Now answer these questions in sentences.
   (a) Why was Cronos so afraid of his own children?
   (b) What did Cronos do because of this fear?
   (c) How did Zeus escape?
   (d) How was Zeus successfully brought up?

2 Write the heading *Zeus Takes Over*. Underline. Answer these questions in sentences.
   (a) How did Zeus and his mother overthrow Cronos?
   (b) Whom did Zeus fight after this?
   (c) Who helped Zeus to win this battle? How?
   (d) What position did Zeus now hold?
   (e) Where did Zeus go to live?

Section B

3 Draw two pictures to illustrate this story. The first picture should illustrate your answers to part 1 (Cronos Rules); the second should illustrate your answers to part 2 (Zeus Takes Over). Colour both pictures and give each of them a title.

3 The Gods of Olympus

Mount Olympus

Zeus was now King of all the gods and lived on Mount Olympus. The other gods lived there too at the court of Zeus and there, when they were not quarrelling, they had their feasts. They ate a special food, called ambrosia, and drank a honey-sweet drink, nectar. The gods looked very much like humans but in their veins, instead of blood, flowed a special liquid, ichor, which helped to make them immortal. There were many different gods and goddesses, each with special powers and duties.

These gods may seem strange to us now but the early Greeks believed that they were all-powerful. It is not hard to understand why.

A great storm might blow up at sea with gale-force winds and mighty waves over 10 metres high. These waves might engulf a small ship and send it crashing to the bottom of the sea with the loss of all the sailors. The Greeks could not explain why such a disaster could happen. To them, this seemed to be the work of some super-being with enormous powers who could

Apollo, god
of the sun
and prophecy

Zeus, king
of the gods
and god
of the sky

Hades, god
of the dead

Hera, queen
of the gods

Athena,
goddess
of wisdom

Aphrodite,
goddess of
love

Artemis,
goddess of
hunting and
the moon

Hermes,
messenger
of the gods

Eros, god
of love

Poseidon,
god of the
sea

Demeter,
goddess of
the earth
and the crops

Hestia,
goddess of
the hearth

Hephaestus,
god of fire

Dionysus,
god of wine

Ares, god
of war

The gods of Olympus

10

make the winds blow fiercely and set the sea rising high in
monstrous waves. This super-being, with his frightening
powers, could only be a god.

This was the only way in which the Greeks could explain
the events which happened in the world about them. The gods
were really the powers of nature: Zeus was the great expanse
of the sky and the bright flash of lightning; Apollo represented

Poseidon

Athena

Hermes

the warmth and energy of the sun; Poseidon stood for the mighty power of the sea; Ares was the terrible destruction of war; Demeter, the fertile mother goddess, was the fruitful earth which produces crops and fruits every year; Aphrodite was the power of love and beauty; Dionysus represented the strange power of wine; Hephaestus was the power and energy of fire; Hades was the dark mystery of Death.

So, all the early Greeks, for generation after generation, saw their gods as explanations of the powers of nature and of the mighty elements that surrounded them. We try to explain such things (for example, a flash of lightning, a storm at sea) by scientific methods. To the early Greeks they were awesome examples of the gods' power.

People bringing offerings to Artemis

The Roman Gods

About 150 years before the birth of Christ, the descendants of these early Greeks were conquered by the Romans. The conquerors admired the Greeks and their many, wonderful achievements so much that they tried to copy all that was best in the Greek way of life. It is not surprising, therefore, that they copied many of the Greek stories about the gods and goddesses. They even identified some of the Greek gods with their own gods who had similar powers. The list on the next page will help you to identify the gods who were alike.

11

Greek	Roman
Cronos	Saturn
Zeus	Jupiter
Hera	Juno
Poseidon	Neptune
Demeter	Ceres
Hestia	Vesta
Hades	Dis
Athena	Minerva
Ares	Mars
Apollo	Apollo
Artemis	Diana
Aphrodite	Venus
Eros	Cupid
Hermes	Mercury
Dionysus	Bacchus *or* Liber
Hephaestus	Vulcan

Temple to Poseidon at Sounion

The gods were subject to much the same emotions as humans —love and friendship, hate and enmity, jealousy and spite. Often they could not resist meddling in the affairs of humans, controlling men as we might control and move chess-pieces. During the great war between the Greeks and the Trojans, the gods took sides, some supporting the Greeks, some supporting the Trojans. In this excerpt from the *Iliad*, the epic poem by Homer about the Trojan War, the gods are discussing what to do while a temporary truce is in operation.

The gods, meanwhile, had sat down for a conference with Zeus in the Hall of the Golden Floor. The Lady Hebe, acting as their cupbearer, served them with nectar, and they drank each other's health from tankards of gold as they looked out on the city of Troy.

By way of tormenting Hera, the Son of Cronos opened in a sarcastic vein. 'Two of the goddesses,' he slyly observed, 'are on Menelaus' side, Hera of Argos and Alalcomenean Athena. But I note that they sit idle here and are content to watch; whereas laughter-loving Aphrodite always keeps close to Paris and shields him from calamity. Only a moment ago she whisked him off when he thought his end had come. Nevertheless, victory has certainly gone to Menelaus, favourite of Ares, and it remains for us to consider what shall happen next. Are we to stir up this wicked strife again, with all the sound and fury of war; or shall we make the Trojans and Achaeans friends? Subject to your approval this would mean that King

Priam's city would survive and Menelaus take Argive Helen back.'

This speech drew muttered protests from Athena and Hera, who were sitting together, plotting evil for the Trojans. However, Athena held her tongue, for all her annoyance with her Father, Zeus. She made no rejoinder, though she seethed with indignation. But Hera could not contain her rage, and burst into speech. 'Dread Son of Cronos, what you propose is monstrous! How can you think of making all my labour null and void, the pains I took, the sweat that poured from me while my horses toiled around as I was gathering the clans to make trouble for Priam and his sons? Do as you please; but do not imagine that all the rest of us approve.'

Zeus the Cloud-gatherer fiercely resented this. 'Madam,' he said, 'what injury can Priam and his sons have done you to account for the vehemence of your desire to sack the lovely town of Troy? Will nothing satisfy your malice but to storm the gates and the long walls and eat up Priam and his sons and all his people raw? Act as you see fit—I do not wish this difference of ours to grow into a serious breach. But there is one condition that I make—remember it. When it is *my* turn to desire the downfall of a town and I choose one where friends of yours are living, make no attempt to curb my anger, but let me have my way, since I have given in to you this time of my own accord, though much against my inclination. For of all the cities that men live in under the sun and starry sky, the nearest to my heart was holy Ilium, with Priam and the people of Priam of the good ashen spear. Never at their banquets did my altar go without its proper share of wine and fat, the offerings that we claim as ours.'

'The three towns *I* love best,' the ox-eyed Queen of Heaven replied, 'are Argos, Sparta, and Mycenae of the Broad Streets. Sack those, if ever they become obnoxious to you. I shall not grudge you their destruction nor make a stand on their behalf. Even if I do object and meddle with your plans, I shall achieve nothing—you are far too strong for me. And yet my enterprises ought not to be thwarted any more than yours. For I too am divine and our parentage is one. Of all the children of Cronos of the Crooked Ways, I take precedence, both by right of birth and because I am your Consort and you are King of all the gods. However, by all means let us yield to one another in this matter, I to you and you to me, and the rest of the immortal gods will follow us. All I ask you to do now is to tell Athena to visit the front and arrange for the Trojans to break the truce by an act of aggression against the triumphant Achaeans.'

The Father of men and gods did not demur, and at once made his wishes clear to Athena. 'Off with you to the front,' he said. 'Visit the armies and contrive to make the Trojans break the truce by attacking the Achaeans in their triumph.'

Things to do

Section A

Write as a heading *The Gods of Olympus*. Underline.

1 Look at the pictures of the gods and goddesses on page 10. Write down in your notebook the names of the gods given in the caption to that picture, and then write down the function (or duty) of that god. Write down also his Roman name.

   (e.g. (a) Zeus, King of the Gods and God of the Sky—Jupiter).

2 Choose any four of these gods and goddesses and draw pictures of them in your notebook. Colour your pictures.

3 Copy this sentence into your notebook:

   Most of the Greek gods were really powers of nature.

   Now write a short paragraph to explain what this means, giving examples where possible.

Section B

1 A class activity: make a frieze showing all the gods and goddesses at their home on Mount Olympus.

2 In small groups, with the help of your teacher, you could choose the gods you like most and make life-size drawings of them to decorate your classroom.

3 Choose some force or element in nature and invent your own god as an explanation of it. Give the god a name and draw a picture of him.

4 Compose a prayer to one of the gods asking for help:

   e.g. to Poseidon for a safe voyage;

   to Demeter for a successful harvest;

   to Ares for victory in battle.

5 Find out the meaning of these English words and note down how they are connected with the gods:

   cereal; martial; volcano; erotic.

6 Many trade-mark names have been borrowed from the names of the Greek gods. Can you think of any? Design

an advertisement for such a product, using a Greek theme as part of the design.

7 The three largest planets of the Solar System are Jupiter, Uranus and Saturn. Why were these particular names chosen?

4 The Other Gods and Goddesses

Naiads

Nymphs

As well as the mighty gods of Mount Olympus the Greeks believed in many less important gods. Living in every river there was a strong god with the horns of an ox, and there were dozens of lovely goddesses called Naiads in charge of fresh-water fountains and springs. An ordinary human always had to ask their permission before drinking any water from a fountain or spring. Many other goddesses, the Nereids (something like our mermaids) lived in the salt-water of the ocean and obeyed their master, the sea-god Poseidon.

Every wood and forest was inhabited by beautiful goddesses, the Nymphs, whose duty it was to protect all the different kinds of trees in the forest. If anyone ever tried to cut down a tree without first sacrificing some animal like a pig to the Nymphs, his axe would bounce off the trunk and cut his own legs.

The Nymphs of the forest were ruled over by the chief god of the countryside, Pan. He always avoided the great Olympian gods but tried hard to protect the shepherds and hunters. One of his favourite occupations was to go dancing in the moonlight with the Nymphs. As he danced he played music on a special instrument made from several wooden pipes and known as the pipes of Pan.

Everyone thought that Pan was very ugly—even his mother was supposed to have run away in terror when she first saw him! He had little curved horns, a small, pointed beard and the legs, hooves and tail of a goat, all covered in fur. The other gods used to laugh at him.

Every afternoon, Pan liked to sleep for a short time in a cave or forest grove. If some traveller chanced upon him and woke him up, Pan would let out a blood-curdling scream and jump about so fiercely that the traveller's hair stood on end, like a hedgehog's bristles. He would be so scared that he would run for his life in what we still call a panic.

Things to do

1 Write the heading *The Other Gods*. Now copy out this paragraph filling in the blanks:

As well as worshipping the great gods of Olympus, the Greeks believed in . . . . Apart from the god Poseidon, several other gods and goddesses were associated with water. Living in every river was . . . . The Naiads were . . . . in charge of . . . . The Nereids were . . . . and lived in . . . . Every wood was inhabited by . . . . whose duty was to . . . . They were ruled over by . . . . the chief god of the countryside.

2 Describe Pan in your own words and draw a picture of him. Colour your picture.

3 What does the word 'panic' mean? Why does it have this meaning?

Pan

5 Kidnap!

The Greeks had many gods; most of them were really explanations of the powers of nature. The Greeks also told many stories about their gods, or about how the gods behaved towards human beings, and many of these stories are also attempts to explain some power or force in nature that mystified the early Greeks.

One such story was told to explain an event in nature which happens every year and which always amazed the Greeks, just as it still amazes people today. This story is given below. Read it and see if you can find out what it is trying to explain.

Hades was the dark and gloomy god of the Underworld, the Land of the Dead. He never smiled and was never happy. Nobody liked him. He longed to have a wife to sit by his side as queen, but no woman, no goddess even, would marry him. In desperation Hades decided to act. He yoked his horses to his black chariot and thundered up to earth looking for a wife.

Near Athens he spotted Persephone, the daughter of Demeter (goddess of crops and fruits). Persephone was picking some flowers and in the bright sunshine looked very beautiful. Hades decided to take Persephone to be his wife. So he snatched her up and carried her away in his chariot. Persephone screamed but it was no use. Her friends rushed up to the spot but too late—Persephone was gone, leaving no trace behind her except some crushed daisies.

Left to right: Hades; Persephone picking flowers; Hades seizes Persephone; young man tells Demeter of the kidnap

Hades kidnaps Persephone

When Demeter heard that Persephone was missing she was heart-broken. For a long time she wandered all over Greece looking for her daughter, asking if anyone had seen her. At last a young man came to her and said that his brother had heard the thunder of hooves and had seen a chariot rush past. In the chariot he had seen a frightened young girl and a wild-eyed man who drove his horses on as fast as the wind. Then the earth gaped open and down the chariot rushed. The earth quickly closed again, leaving no trace of what had happened.

Demeter now knew that the dark-faced king must have been Hades. She blamed Zeus for what had happened and swore to get her own back. She put a curse on all the countryside so that no tree bore fruit, no corn grew for men to eat, no grass for the cattle. Zeus was worried since the whole earth started to die. He offered Demeter wonderful presents but she refused to lift her curse unless Persephone was restored to her. Eventually Zeus agreed to do this. He told Demeter: 'Persephone will be returned to you, but on one condition—she must not yet have eaten the food of the Dead.'

Left to right: The curse of Demeter; Demeter and Zeus; Hades with pomegranate; Persephone and Demeter together

Zeus ordered Hades to release Persephone on this one condition. Hades reluctantly sent for Persephone and said: 'What is wrong, my dear? Why are you so unhappy? You seem to be pining away. You must eat something.' But all Persephone could do was cry. Hades sighed and looked gloomier than ever.

'Maybe you'd better go home to your mother,' he muttered.

For the first time in many months Persephone smiled. Her ordeal was over; but at that very moment one of Hades' gardeners burst out into a loud laugh.

'Why, don't let her fool you, sire! This very morning I saw her with my own eyes picking a pomegranate from your orchard. She ate five of the seeds!'

Hades smiled to himself, for now Persephone would have to stay with him. Demeter was shocked when she heard the sad news and screamed out: 'If she stays with Hades, I shall never lift my curse from the Earth. Everything on it, animals, plants, will die!'

In the end, Zeus had to devise this plan to suit Demeter: Persephone was to marry Hades and spend five months of the year in Tartarus, the Underworld (one month for each pomegranate seed eaten). For the remaining seven months she was allowed to return to her mother. It was only during these seven months that Demeter lifted her curse and allowed anything to grow on earth.

Hades seizes Persephone

Things to do

Section A

This time the heading is *The Kidnapping of Persephone*. Underline.

1 Imagine that you are Demeter. Tell what has happened to your daughter Persephone, what you did to try and get her back, what solution you finally had to accept.
2 Draw and colour a small cartoon-strip to illustrate the various stages of the story.
3 What event in nature is this story trying to explain?

Section B

1 With some of your friends write a short play about the kidnapping. Act the play out to the rest of the class. Perhaps your teacher could record the play with suitable sound effects and background music.

20

6 The Pain of Love

Have you ever wondered why the daffodil always hangs its head as if looking for something, while most other flowers raise their heads to the sun? Have you ever wondered why your voice comes back to you when you shout loud in a mountain valley?

The world we live in is full of such wonders. Nature abounds in riddles. Today we can answer these riddles by using scientific methods. The Greeks tried to answer them another way—by telling amazing stories about strange and wonderful people. Here is one such story.

When Narcissus was born his mother went to see a fortune-teller who told her that the boy would live to a ripe, old age—provided that he never saw himself. Narcissus grew up to be very handsome; many women fell in love with him and wanted to marry him, but Narcissus was not interested in them and so he sent them all away.

One of the women who fell in love with Narcissus was a mountain-nymph called Echo. She had once deceived Hera, Queen of the Gods, by telling lies. When Hera found out she punished Echo by taking away her power of speech. All that Echo could do now was to repeat other people's words. This made it very difficult for Echo as she could not tell Narcissus of her love for him. She could never speak to him but only wait for him to speak and then repeat his words.

One day Narcissus went out hunting and soon found himself separated from his companions. Echo, as always, was following him closely, remaining out of sight. Narcissus heard her foot-steps, though, and turned round. He could see no one.

'Is anyone here?' he shouted.

'Here,' repeated Echo.

Narcissus was puzzled. 'Why are you hiding from me?' he cried. Again he heard his own words echoing back. More puzzled than ever he shouted out: 'Come over here! Let us meet!'

Left to right: Echo follows Narcissus; she rushes towards him; Narcissus pushes her away; Echo wastes away

'Let us meet!' said Echo joyfully, as she rushed towards Narcissus, thinking that at last he would return her love. She threw her arms round Narcissus' neck and tried to kiss him.

Narcissus pushed her away and shouted rudely: 'Go away! I'd rather die than let you touch me!' He then turned and ran off home. Poor Echo sank to her knees, tears in her eyes, repeating again and again Narcissus' last words—'Touch me . . . touch me . . . touch me . . .'.

Ever since that day Echo hid herself away in lonely mountain caves. She still loved Narcissus and began to waste away in longing for him. She became thin and wrinkled, and all the freshness of her beauty withered into the air. Soon only her voice remained, haunting with her cries the lonely mountains.

Narcissus continued to live as before, unmoved by poor Echo's plight. He rejected all the people who fell in love with his handsome features. At last, in bitter despair, one of the rejected suitors prayed to the gods that Narcissus should suffer just as she had suffered: 'May he fall in love with someone as I have with him, and may he too be unable to gain his loved one.' The prayer was granted.

One day, while Narcissus was out hunting, he felt thirsty. He soon came to a small pool of clear, fresh water, and knelt down to drink. As he did so, for the first time in his life, he saw his own face—reflected in the still water. He admired the handsome face that so many had loved in vain. Without knowing who it was, and not realizing what was happening, he fell in love with the face and lay there for hours gazing into the pool. Time and time again Narcissus tried to kiss the face, but he only got wet and spoilt the reflection. No thought of food or rest could draw him away, so much did he long to touch that face. At last, in despair and disappointment, able to stand the frustration no longer, he pulled his dagger from his belt and plunged it deep into his chest.

Echo, who was now invisible, stood nearby watching what was happening and pitying Narcissus in her heart.

'Alas,' said Narcissus as he gazed into the pool for the last time.

'Alas,' Echo sighed as she watched helplessly.

'Farewell, farewell,' groaned Narcissus as he finally died.

'Farewell, farewell,' came Echo's voice.

Narcissus was gone forever, but from the spot on the ground where his blood had fallen there sprang up a white narcissus flower, which still hangs its head sadly, looking at its reflection in mountain pools.

(Adapted from Ovid 'Metamorphoses')

Left to right: Narcissus sees his reflection; he tries to kiss it; he pulls out his knife; Narcissus dying

Things to do

Section A

Write the heading *Narcissus and Echo*. Underline.

1 In your own words briefly tell the story of Narcissus and Echo. This skeleton of the story will help you:

Narcissus born—fortune-teller—never see himself—very handsome—rejects all women—Echo—her punishment—love for Narcissus—her meeting with Narcissus—her rejection and suffering—prayer against Narcissus—Narcissus out hunting—thirst—pool of water—reflection—suicide—flower.

2 What is the connection between the events of this story and
(a) the daffodil's drooping head;
(b) your voice coming back to you in a mountain valley?

3 Design *either* a poster to advertise a feature film based on the story of Narcissus and Echo;
or a jacket cover for a book which tells this story.

Section B

Here is a short poem by the English poet and Greek scholar A. E. Housman. Read it carefully and answer the questions which follow.

Look not in my eyes, for fear
  They mirror true the sight I see
And there you find your face too clear
  And love it and be lost like me.
One the long night through must lie
  Spent in star-defeated sighs,
But why should you as well as I
  Perish? Gaze not in my eyes.

A Grecian lad, as I hear tell,
  One that many loved in vain,
Looked into a forest well
  And never looked away again.
There, where the turf in springtime flowers,
  With downward eye and gazes sad,
Stands amid the glancing showers
  A jonquil, not a Grecian lad.

1 Who is the Grecian lad?
2 Who loved him in vain?
3 The jonquil, the daffodil and the narcissus are all flowers
   of the same type. Draw and colour such a flower. Why is
   its head said to droop?
4 How is the first verse of this poem connected to the second?
5 Compose a short poem of your own to tell the story of
   Narcissus and Echo.

24

7 Man is Created

The Titans, led by Cronos, had ruled the world until Zeus attacked his father and seized power for himself and the other Olympian gods. After his victory, Zeus banished the Titans. Atlas, the leader of Cronos' defeated army, was condemned by Zeus to support the sky on his shoulders until the end of the world. Only two of the Titans were spared any punishment —Prometheus (a name which means 'Forethought') and his brother Epimetheus (which means 'Afterthought'). Prometheus had warned the other Titans that Zeus would win the war; he had actually fought for Zeus and had persuaded his brother to do the same.

Although Prometheus had helped Zeus, he soon displeased the mighty king. Once a dispute arose as to which parts of a sacrificed bull should be offered to the gods, and which parts kept by men. Prometheus was asked to decide. He had made the first race of men, by moulding them out of river mud just as a potter uses clay, and he wanted to help them, if he could. He killed a bull and cut it up. He put the pieces into two bags. In one bag he placed all the good meat but this he covered with tripe, the stomach of the animal, which no one likes. In the other bag, which was bigger, he placed all the bones and, on top to conceal them, he placed a rich layer of fat. He then asked Zeus to choose which bag he preferred. Zeus foolishly chose the bigger bag where all the bones were hidden. The other bag with the good meat was then given to men. Zeus was furious when he realized that he had been cheated, and so he stopped men receiving the gift of fire—the first step towards civilization. 'Let them eat their meat raw!' he thundered.

Atlas supporting the sky

Prometheus was very disappointed. He did not want the creatures he had made to be hurt in any way, and so he decided to disobey Zeus and give fire to men. He secretly entered Olympus and stole a glowing coal from Hestia's fire. He carried it down to earth and showed the humans how to use it. They would now be able to cook their meat, keep themselves warm and protect themselves from wild animals.

Left to right: Zeus overthrows Cronos and the giants; Prometheus models man from clay; he gives fire to man

Zeus was angry when he found out what Prometheus had done. He wanted revenge and so he decided to punish the men made by Prometheus. He knew that Prometheus had collected all the evils and germs which might harm men and had locked them all away in a large box. If the box were ever opened all the evil things would fly out and attack mankind. Zeus devised a clever plan to get the box open.

He ordered Hephaestus to make a clay figure. Zeus gave the figure life and called it Woman—the first woman ever made. The goddesses gave her all their graces and called her Pandora ('All-gifts'). Zeus now sent her to Prometheus' brother, the slow-witted Epimetheus. As soon as he saw her, Epimetheus, bewitched by her beauty, fell in love and wanted to marry her. Prometheus suspected that this was a trick and ordered Epimetheus to send her back.

Zeus was angrier than ever now that his plan had failed. He even accused Prometheus of trying to assault Athena and as a punishment he chained Prometheus to a rock in the Caucasus Mountains. As he lay there helpless, a huge vulture came and tore at his liver. At night the vulture went away and the liver healed. But on the next day the vulture returned; and so Prometheus suffered, day after day, for all time.

Epimetheus was shocked by his brother's harsh treatment and frightened that he would suffer the same. He therefore married Pandora and took her home. One day Pandora found the box hidden away in a cupboard. Although Epimetheus had

Left to right: Prometheus with box of evil things; Epimetheus meets Pandora; Prometheus being punished; Pandora opens the box

told her never to touch that box, she opened it—as Zeus had intended her to do all along. Out, in a swarm came all the evil things which make life difficult for men—old age, sickness, plague, famine, hate, spite, enmity and jealousy. Prometheus' men, who till now had led happy lives free from worry and disease, now began to suffer terribly. Only the last creature out of the box—Hope—kept the men from killing themselves in despair.

Things to do

Section A

Write the heading *Prometheus and Pandora*. Underline.
1 Below is a skeleton framework of the story. Use this to write your own account of the story. Include as many details as you can.

War between Zeus and Titans—Titans lose and are punished—Prometheus spared—Prometheus makes men—Dispute over sacrifice—Prometheus' actions displease Zeus—Zeus' plan for revenge—Pandora, the first woman—Epimetheus' love—Prometheus' punishment—Epimetheus' frightened actions—Pandora finds the box—All the evils of the world.
2 Draw and colour a picture of (a) Prometheus being punished; (b) Pandora opening the box.

Section B

1 What story from another culture does this story remind you of?
2 What do you think the Greeks were trying to explain in this story?
3 Why were the names given to Prometheus and Epimetheus particularly suitable?
4 Do you think Zeus was justified in punishing Prometheus, or was he too harsh?
5 Write a conversation between Zeus and Prometheus in which Zeus accuses Prometheus of a crime, with Prometheus defending his actions.

8 Prayer and Sacrifice

(a) Festivals for the Gods

The worship of the gods was very important to the Ancient Greeks. They believed that the gods were all-powerful and that they controlled everything which happened in their lives. Without the help of the gods they could never be successful or happy. The gods, therefore, had to be treated with great respect and worshipped in the correct way.

The gods controlled not only the lives of every man but also the affairs of all cities, each of which had its own god or goddess to protect it. Everyone in the city was openly involved in the worship of the god. Festivals were held to honour the god, and his help was sought in matters important to the city like trade or war. The special goddess who protected Athens was Athena, after whom the city was called. She had once competed with Poseidon to see who should control Athens. The city was to be given to the one who gave the people the more useful gift. Poseidon struck a rock with his trident and from it gushed a salt-water spring; Athena produced the olive-tree with its valuable fruit, and she was judged the winner. From then on the city was called Athena's city, or Athens.

Every four years the Athenians held a great festival in honour of Athena. This festival was called the Panathenaea. A great procession wound its way through the streets of the city, making its way to the Parthenon, the great temple built in honour of Athena on top of the Acropolis, a high, rocky hill in the centre of the city. There, animals were sacrificed to the goddess and a beautiful robe, embroidered in gold with scenes from ancient legends, was draped round the huge statue of Athena inside the temple. During the procession the robe had been hoisted up like a sail on the mast of a ship which was pulled through the streets on wheels. The Athenians also held music and athletic competitions at this time to honour the goddess who protected the city.

Contest between Athena and Poseidon

28

The Panathenaic procession

Perhaps the most famous of all the festivals in honour of the gods took place at Olympia in southern Greece. There, every four years, people gathered from all over the Greek world to worship Zeus, the greatest of the gods. Athletic and music

Zeus at Olympia

29

A race at the ancient Olympics

contests were organized in honour of the god. From these developed our modern Olympic games, a festival of sport and friendship.

Opening procession at modern Olympics

Things to do

Section A

Put the heading *Festivals for the Gods*. Underline. Copy these passages into your notebook, filling in the blanks:

1 The ancient Greeks believed that the gods were . . . .
Without the help of the gods they could never be . . . .
Therefore, the gods had to be . . . .

2 The gods controlled the affairs of every man and also of
. . . . Each . . . . had a god or goddess to . . . . . .
The goddess who protected Athens was . . . .

3 Every . . . . years the Panathenaea took place. This
was a . . . . in honour of . . . . Animals were
. . . . and the statue of the goddess was . . . . At
this time the Athenians also held . . . .

4 Perhaps the most famous festival was held at . . . . in
honour of . . . . To honour the god the people
organized . . . . and . . . . contests. This ancient
festival was the origin of our modern festival of . . . .
and . . . . , the . . . . Games.

Section B

1 Draw and colour a picture of the Panathenaea.
2 Imagine that you are present in Athens as the Panathenaea takes place. You are a radio commentator for the BBC. In your own words, write down the commentary which you would use to describe the scene for the audience at home.

(b) Temples

The Parthenon in Athens was the great temple dedicated to Athena, the goddess who protected the city. It is still standing today and from its position high on the Acropolis it keeps eternal watch over the city. Every year it is visited by thousands of tourists who all admire its grace and beauty.

Above: The Parthenon today

Left: The Acropolis as it may have been

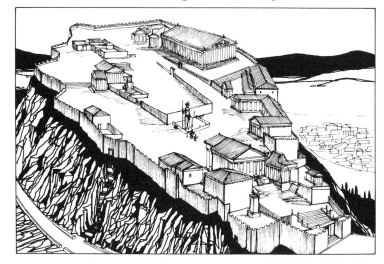

The statue of Athena

Such temples were built in every part of the Greek world. Inside there was usually a large statue of the god or goddess to whom the temple was dedicated. In Athens, on the Acropolis, there was also a large statue of Athena *outside* the temple.

Early temples were built of wood but later stone or marble was used instead, because it was much stronger. Unlike modern churches the worshippers did not go inside the temple as a group but gathered just outside to pray and to make their offerings to the god. (Anyone wishing closer contact with the god might enter the temple and pray there on his own.) The offerings were often large sums of money or valuable pieces of gold or silver. These were kept in a special strong-room at the back of the temple. Often an animal was sacrificed and offered to the god.

31

Temple of Hephaestus, Athens

Temple of Demeter at Paestum, South Italy

South American Aztecs also made sacrifices to their gods as the stone shows

Things to do

Section A

The section heading is *Temples*. Answer these questions in sentences:

1 Look at the top picture on page 31:
Which building does the picture show?
What was the building used for?
Where can you still see the remains of this building?
Draw or trace a picture of the building. Colour your drawing.
2 What would you have found inside the temple? Draw and colour a picture to illustrate your answer.
3 What were early temples made of?
4 What was used later and why?
5 Where did the people worshipping the god usually stand?
6 Why was a strong-room necessary in many temples?

Section B

1 Collect old postcards, or photographs from travel-brochures, which show Greek temples. Paste them into your notebook.
2 Many buildings all over the world have been built according to the Greek style. Can you think of any near you? Describe such a building in your notebook and draw a picture of it. Perhaps you could even take a photograph of it and paste this into a notebook.

(c) Sacrifices

The Greek prayed to their gods, standing upright. They raised their arms to the sky, with the palms of their hands turned upwards. If they were praying to the gods of the Underworld, they kept their palms turned downwards. Combined with the prayer there was often a sacrifice, when an animal was killed and offered to a god to please him. In early times a human being may have been sacrificed but later animals were killed and offered to the gods in order to thank them for some success or to ask for help.

The priest and his attendants, with garlands in their hair and dressed in white, gathered near to the god's temple to

Heifer being led to sacrifice

perform the sacrifice. Everyone present was sprinkled with purified water. The priest called for silence and the correct prayers were said.

The animal was then led to the altar. The victim was usually a sheep or an ox but some gods demanded specific types of victims. Horses were sacrificed to Poseidon; pigs to Demeter and Dionysus; goats to Hera and Artemis. It was the custom to sacrifice male animals to gods and female animals to goddesses. Animals with dark coats or skins were usually sacrificed to the gods of the Underworld.

Barley grains were sprinkled over the head and body of the victim, and a few hairs were cut from the forehead and thrown into the fire as a sort of first offering. The beast was then killed with an axe, or stunned with a club. Its throat was cut and the blood was caught in a bowl. The blood was sprinkled over the altar and sometimes even over the worshippers. During the ceremony all the people shouted loudly and music was played on the flute.

The victim was immediately cut up. The entrails were examined carefully to see if the future could be foretold. The thigh-bones were wrapped in fat and burned on the altar as a special offering to the gods. The rest of the meat was used to provide a feast for all the people at the· sacrifice who seldom tasted beef except on such an occasion.

Things to do

Write the heading *Sacrifices*. Underline. Answer these questions in sentences.

1 How did the Greeks pray?
2 What was a sacrifice?
3 Why did the Greeks perform sacrifices?
4 What did the Greeks sacrifice?
5 You are a journalist writing articles on strange customs in other lands. You have been allowed to attend a sacrifice in Ancient Greece. Describe carefully and accurately what you saw. Draw a picture which is meant (as a photograph) to accompany your article.

(d) Tinker, tailor . . .

Would you like to know what will happen to you in the future? Have you ever read your horoscope in a newspaper or magazine to see what awaits you in the days ahead? Maybe someone at a

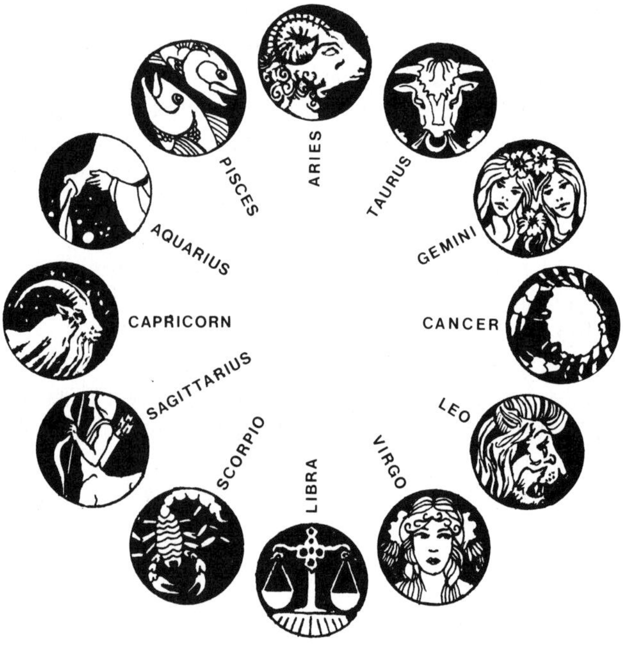

The signs of the zodiac

PISCES
ARIES
TAURUS
AQUARIUS
GEMINI
CAPRICORN
CANCER
SAGITTARIUS
LEO
SCORPIO
LIBRA
VIRGO

fairground has tried to read your fortune. People have always been interested in finding out what the future holds for them. Some think that the future lies in the stars; others prefer to read the future in the palm of your hand; a few still believe that the future can be foretold from the pattern of the tea-leaves in a cup!

Many people in ancient times also tried to see into the future and thought that they could forecast what was going to happen. Most people believed in omens—signs which could forecast good or bad luck. Perhaps you consider it a good omen if a black cat walks across your path or if you find a four-leaf clover. For the ancient Greeks, the flight of a bird, a peal of thunder, a flash of lightning were seen as omens—vultures on the left were unlucky; the cry of a heron or a flash of lightning were considered lucky. The entrails of a sacrificed animal were also inspected carefully for omens.

Gypsy looking into a crystal ball

Left: Clay model of sheep's liver, used for prediction

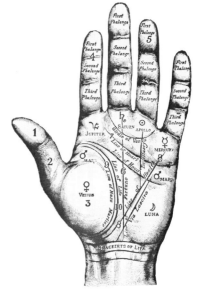

The god responsible for predicting future events (a skill called prophecy) was Apollo. He had a famous temple at Delphi, a place surrounded by sheer mountains, which was considered by the Greeks to be the centre of the earth.

Those who wished to seek the advice of the god gathered at Delphi. There they made valuable offerings to the god,

35

Ruins of Apollo's temple at Delphi

The priestess at Delphi accompaniec by priests

including the sacrifice of a goat, in the hope that the god would be pleased and give a favourable reply. The priestess of Apollo, known as the Pythia, then prepared to contact the god.

She purified herself in a fresh-water spring which ran nearby. Then, accompanied by priests, she withdrew to an underground room. There she worked herself up into a state of frenzy. Some say that she did this by breathing in fumes which came up from a rift in the rock. It may be that the priestess, like a spiritualist medium today, believed so strongly in her power to contact the god that it was easy for her to go into a trance. She may also have chewed certain leaves which contained a mild form of some drug.

After contacting the god she eventually gave the god's reply in the form of a riddle which the priest in attendance would explain, usually in verse. Sometimes the answer would have two meanings. Perhaps the most famous reply was given to King Croesus, the ruler of Lydia (part of the country we now call Turkey). Croesus, one of the richest men in the ancient world, brought valuable offerings for the god, hoping for a favourable reply to his question. He wanted to find out whether or not he would be successful if he attacked his neighbours, the Persians, by crossing over the river Halys, the boundary of his empire. He received this reply:

> When Croesus has the Halys crossed
> A mighty empire will be lost.

Croesus went away, happy with the reply and confident of success. He attacked his neighbours and by so doing destroyed his *own* empire!

Things to do

Section A

The heading this time is *Telling the Future*. Underline. Write in your notebook the following sentences, filling in the blank spaces with the correct word or phrase. Choose these words or phrases from the jumbled list given below.

1 Many people in the ancient World, including the early Greeks, tried to . . . .
2 The god of prophecy was . . . .
3 Prophecy is . . . .
4 The god of prophecy had a beautiful temple at . . . .
5 His priestess was called . . . .
6 Those seeking advice from the god sacrificed . . . .
7 The priestess, after purifying herself, contacted the god by . . . .
8 The priestess gave the reply in . . . .
9 The reply was explained by . . . .
10 The answers often . . . .

---

working herself up into a state of frenzy; Apollo; the form of a riddle; the Pythia; see into the future; had two meanings; a priest; a goat; Delphi; predicting future events.

Section B

1 Draw and colour a picture of the priestess at Delphi.
2 Compose a riddling reply to a question which can be interpreted in two ways.
3 The early Greeks were very superstitious, just as many people still are today. The title of this section is part of a superstitious belief. Can you complete it and say what it refers to? Write down any other superstitions that you know.

9 The Great Flood

Deucalion, King of Phthia, was the son of Prometheus. One day he went to visit his father in the Caucasus Mountains and he tried to drive off the vulture that was feeding on his liver. During a short break in the vulture's attacks, Prometheus warned his son that a terrible flood was about to happen. Deucalion believed his father, who could see into the future, and so he hurried away home. He built a boat or ark, and he and his wife Pyrrha hurried on board, taking with them all their possessions and farm animals. They settled down in the ark and waited for the flood to come.

About the same time Zeus had been travelling on earth disguised as a poor man. He was shocked at all the crimes committed by man, and especially by the people of Arcadia whose King offered Zeus a dish containing human flesh. In disgust and anger Zeus blasted the King's palace with his thunderbolts and turned the King into a wolf. He thought that this was a good time to punish all the rest of mankind for their crimes. He could not use his usual weapon, the thunderbolt, all over the world in case he set the upper air ablaze. So, on this occasion, he decided on a different punishment—to send rain pouring down from every quarter of the sky and so destroy mankind beneath the floodwaters.

He made the South wind blow and the rain began to fall, at first gently but then in great torrents. Poseidon, Zeus' brother, helped by sending the rivers crashing over their banks to flood the surrounding countryside. All the buildings and temples were washed away. Sea and earth could no longer be distinguished; all was sea, and a sea that had no shores. Some people tried to escape by climbing to the hilltops, others by sitting in their curved boats. Some people plied the oars where only recently they had been ploughing; some sailed over cornland, over the submerged roofs of their homes, while some found fish in the topmost branches of the elms. The ocean overwhelmed the hills, and waves were washing against the

mountain peaks. Nearly the whole human race was swallowed up by the waters: those whom the sea spared died from the lack of food, overcome by hunger.

Deucalion's boat rose with the floodwaters and drifted for nine days. Thanks to his father's warning, Deucalion had enough food aboard so that he and his wife did not go hungry. On the ninth day, when Zeus saw that almost everyone had perished, he stopped the rain falling and allowed the flood water to subside. As the earth began to reappear, Deucalion steered his boat to the nearest land. His boat finally came to rest near Mount Parnassus.

Deucalion and his wife quickly left the boat and immediately sacrificed one of their rams, kept safe in the ark with them, to Zeus, asking that mankind should be reborn. Zeus heard their prayer and, realizing that Deucalion and Pyrrha were good, god-fearing people, he sent Hermes to tell them that their prayer would be granted if they followed Zeus' instructions. These instructions were like a riddle: 'Cover your heads and throw the bones of your mother behind you!'

Deucalion and Pyrrha wondered what this could mean. They both had different mothers and both were dead, buried in graveyards now submerged beneath the flood-waters. So what could Zeus mean? They guessed that by 'mother' he meant Mother Earth, whose bones were the rocks lying around them. They covered their heads and picked up some rocks which they threw behind them. The rocks turned into men and women

Left to right: Prometheus warns his son of the flood; Deucalion builds the ark; the heavens open; the flood waters rise

Left to right: Deucalion's ark rises with the flood; the flood subsides —land appears; Deucalion praises Zeus; Deucalion and Pyrrha throw the rocks behind them

as they touched the ground. Thus the human race was reborn. Deucalion and Pyrrha also had a naturally born son of their own. They called him Hellen and it is from his name that the Greeks still call themselves Hellenes.

Things to do

Section A

Write the heading *The Great Flood*. Underline.
1   Imagine that you are Deucalion and are now an old man. You have been asked by a grandson to tell the story of the flood which happened a long time ago. Tell your story.
2   Draw and colour pictures of the ark with all the animals being loaded on and off the ark at the height of the storm.

Section B

1   What story from another culture does this story remind you of? Find out as much as you can about this other story.
2   What does the fact that two different cultures have almost identical stories about a flood tell us?

10 The Dead

(a) Funeral customs

What happens to humans after they die? People have always been fascinated by this question. Many believe that there is a life after death. Some experts believe that they can actually contact and speak to the spirits of this after-life. Belief in the after-life is not new—it is thousands of years old.

The people of Ancient Egypt believed so strongly in a life after death that they preserved the bodies of the dead. This was so that the soul of the dead man could recognize its original body in the next world. A body preserved by the Egyptians is called a mummy.

The Ancient Greeks also believed in a life after death. Although they did not preserve the body like the Egyptians or have such elaborate burial customs, they were still very careful that the dead body was disposed of in the proper way, with great respect and due funeral rites.

The body was washed and dressed in normal, everyday clothes. A coin was placed in the mouth and, after a short period of 'lying in state' when people came to pay their last respects, the body was carried away on a cart or on the shoulders

A mummified cat

Skeleton with a coin in his mouth

A gold funeral mask from Mycenae

A funeral urn

of friends, while the mourners followed. Sometimes the body was buried in the ground or placed in a stone tomb. Valuable gifts and possessions of the dead man were buried with the body, and occasionally, especially among the early Greeks such as those in the great city of Mycenae, a gold death-mask might be placed over the face of a dead king. Several such masks were found by archaeologists at Mycenae. Tombs were usually marked with a simple stone slab on which there was a short inscription.

At other times the Greeks burned or cremated the dead. The body was placed on a funeral pyre, along with gifts and possessions of the dead person. The pyre was then set alight and the body was burned. The ashes were collected in a small vase or urn.

Whatever methods the Greeks used, they considered it vitally important that the body should receive some form of burial ceremony, even if it were just three handfuls of earth scattered over the body as a token of burial. Without such a ceremony the soul of the dead man could not cross over to the after-life but was forced to roam this earth, an unhappy ghost. Only criminals and other unpopular people were left unburied.

Things to do

Use the heading *Funeral Customs*. Underline. Answer these questions in sentences.
1 Did the ancient Greeks believe in a life after death?
2 How did the Greeks dispose of dead bodies? Describe the two methods.
3 Why did the Greeks consider it vitally important for the dead to be buried properly?

Now draw and colour the mask from Mycenae. Say what it was used for.

(b) Land of the Dead

After the ceremony of burial or cremation had been properly carried out, the souls of the dead were led by Hermes to the entrance of the Underworld, the Land of the Dead. This land

Charon rowing boat across the Styx

lay deep beneath the earth and was ruled over by King Hades and his reluctant queen Persephone. After reaching the entrance, Hermes led them down a dark tunnel to the river Styx. There they paid Charon, the old, bearded ferry-man, to row them across, using the coins which relations had placed beneath the tongues of their corpses. Sailors, who might be drowned at sea, far from their homes with no relations to place a coin beneath their tongue, carried their fee for Charon in the form of a piece of gold made into an ear-ring. After crossing the Styx, the dead became ghosts. Those with no coin were left to shiver forever on the riverbank. Some who had escaped from Hermes might succeed in creeping down to the Underworld through a back entrance where no fee was charged, but this entrance was very difficult to find.

On the other side of the river Styx, the main entrance to Hades' dark kingdom was guarded by an enormous three-headed dog called Cerberus. This monster was always awake and on watch. He let no ghosts escape from the dark realm and prevented any mortal still alive from entering.

The ghosts were first sent to the three judges of the dead: Rhadamanthys, who judged the souls from the east; Aeacus

Cerberus

43

The three judges of the dead

who judged those from the west; and Minos, who passed judgment on all the difficult cases.

Those whose lives had been neither very good nor very bad were sent to the Asphodel Fields, a place where the ghosts wandered endlessly, twittering like bats, with nothing to do.

Those who had been very good were sent to Elysium (or The Elysian Fields), a paradise land of meadows and orchards where the sun was always shining. There was no rain or cold. Flowers never withered and fruit was always in season. Games, music and fun never stopped.

The very bad people, like criminals, were sent to Tartarus, the land of Punishment. This place was guarded by the three Furies. They were horrible, withered old women, with snakes instead of hair, dog-like heads, wings like bats and bright, burning eyes. They carried torches and whips with metal studs.

Elysium (or the Elysian Fields)

These Furies could also visit earth to punish living mortals who had been cruel to children, to old people or to their parents.

Things to do

Section A

Write the heading *Land of the Dead*. Underline.

1 Here is a list of nine names mentioned in the previous pages. The letters in these names are all mixed up. Try to unscramble the letters to form a name, and write a sentence or two to explain the name you have uncovered.
(a) Ytxs; (b) Adshe; (c) Rufeis; (d) Sarutrat; (e) Remshe; (f) Phasledo; (g) Sylimue; (h) Noharc; (i) Rebrescu.

2 Draw and colour a picture of Cerberus, *or* of Charon.

Section B

Using your imagination and the description in the passage, draw and colour your own picture of the Furies.

(c) Crime and punishment

Men or women who had committed some unpardonable crime were sent to Tartarus to be punished. Tantalus was one such criminal. He was King of Lydia and, thanks to the blessings of

45

Tantalus offers stew to the gods

Tantalus suffers

Zeus, was one of the richest of all men. He was even invited on occasions to attend the feasts of the gods. Yet soon he abused the trust of the gods. He stole ambrosia, the food of the gods, and gave it to ordinary people, hoping to make them immortal like the gods. To make matters worse, he then asked the gods to a banquet. He killed his own son, Pelops, and offered the gods a sort of cannibal-stew made from his son's body! All the gods realized what was in the stew and refused to eat it. Only Demeter, still grieving over the loss of her daughter Persephone, tasted the meat, chewing on a piece of shoulder. In anger, at this outrage, Zeus blasted Tantalus with a thunderbolt and restored Pelops to life. His damaged shoulder was replaced with one of ivory.

In the Underworld Tantalus was punished for his crime. He was tied to a pole in a pool of water which reached nearly to his chin. Whenever he felt thirsty, he bent his head to drink, but the water always sank out of reach and he could never get a drop to drink. Over his head, from numerous fruit trees, dangled pears, pomegranates, apples, figs—a tempting selection; but whenever he tried to pluck the fruit, the wind would blow it all away out of reach, leaving Tantalus hungry. Thus Tantalus, as punishment for his terrible crime, was condemned to suffer the ravages of everlasting hunger and thirst.

Another famous criminal to be punished in the Underworld was Sisyphus, King of Corinth. He was one of the most cunning of men and even succeeded in cheating Hades. One day, a river god, Asopus, noticed that his daughter Aegina was missing. He suspected that Sisyphus had kidnapped her and so he came to Corinth to search for her. In fact, Sisyphus had not kidnapped the girl but he knew where she was. When Asopus asked him, Sisyphus refused to tell unless the river god produced a fresh-water spring to supply Corinth with running water. Asopus agreed to do so and Sisyphus then told him about his daughter: Zeus had fallen in love with her and had stolen her away. He even told Asopus where to find them. Zeus was angry with Sisyphus for betraying his secret and he immediately ordered his brother Hades to seize Sisyphus and give him a terrible punishment in the Underworld.

Hades went up to Corinth to claim Sisyphus for his kingdom of death. He carried a pair of handcuffs with which to arrest Sisyphus, but when he produced them Sisyphus asked what they were and how they worked. Hades foolishly showed him by placing them on his own wrists. Sisyphus rushed forward and locked them, thus making Hades his prisoner! This was a ridiculous situation since no one could die while Hades, god of the Dead, was a prisoner on earth—not even men who had been beheaded or cut to pieces. Ares, the god of War, was especially angry since now no one could die in battle! Ares therefore hurried to Corinth to free Hades. He also made sure

Sisyphus laughs at Hades

Sisyphus rolls the boulder up the hill

Dioneus falls into the burning pit

that this time Sisyphus went down to the Underworld with Hades to face his punishment.

Sisyphus, however, was as cunning as ever and first made his wife Merope promise to leave his body unburied. In the Underworld, he complained to Queen Persephone that he had not yet received the proper funeral rites and so should not have been allowed across the river Styx. He asked if he could be allowed to return to earth for a proper burial with a coin beneath his tongue. Persephone, not seeing through his cunning plan, granted his request on condition that he returned within three days. Sisyphus readily made the promise.

On his return to earth Sisyphus promptly forgot his promise to Persephone and refused to go back. He thought that he had cheated death. Eventually Hermes was sent to bring him down at last to the Land of the Dead. This time there was no mistake. Death had claimed him: his life was over.

In the Underworld Sisyphus was punished for giving away Zeus' secret and for trying to cheat death. He was condemned to roll a huge rock up the side of a hill and tumble it down the other side. The great hero Odysseus was once allowed to visit the Underworld, though he was still alive, and he later described Sisyphus' efforts:

I witnessed the torture of Sisyphus, as he tackled his huge rock with both his hands. Leaning against it with his arms and thrusting with his legs, he tried to push the boulder up-hill to the top. But every time, as he was going to send it toppling over the crest, its sheer weight turned it back, and the rock came bounding down again to level ground. So once more he had to wrestle with the thing and push it up, while the sweat poured from his limbs and the dust rose high above his head.

Sisyphus was never to succeed in his efforts.

Ixion, King of the Lapiths, was also punished in Tartarus. He had married Dia, the daughter of Dioneus, and had promised her father many gifts. When Dioneus asked for the gifts, Ixion invited him to dinner. He dug a pit beneath his guest's chair and covered it with branches. In the pit was a fire. When Dioneus sat on the chair his weight sent it crashing through the branches into the pit below where he was burned to death! Zeus actually liked Ixion and forgave him for this crime. He even invited Ixion to one of the gods' feasts. Ixion drank too much and assaulted a woman whom he thought to be the goddess Hera. In fact, it was a woman called Nephele whom Zeus had placed near Ixion on purpose in case something like this happened. Nephele later gave birth to a monstrous creature,

the Centaur, half-man and half-horse. For this second crime, Ixion was sentenced to death. In the Underworld, as a punishment, he was chained to a wheel. This wheel was then lit and sent spinning through the air forever.

Tityus was a giant who once scaled the heights of Olympus and attacked Leto, the mother of the twins Apollo and Artemis. He too was punished in Tartarus—he was chained to the ground while two giant vultures gnawed at his liver.

Perhaps the harshest punishment of all was given to the daughters of Danaus, King of Argos. He had fifty daughters, often called the Danaids. His brother Aegyptus (after whom the country of Egypt is called) had fifty sons. The two brothers quarrelled over their inheritance. Aegyptus suggested that the problem could be solved by uniting the two families in marriage: Danaus' fifty daughters would marry Aegyptus' fifty sons. Danaus suspected some treachery but he was forced to agree to the proposal. During the wedding-feast, Danaus, still suspicious and fearing for his daughters' safety, gave each of his daughters a long, sharp pin which they hid in their hair. That evening, they were to stab their new husbands through the heart.

Forty-nine of the girls obeyed their father and killed their husbands. One of the daughters spared her husband's life and helped him to escape. Although the girls had murdered their cousins, they were forgiven by Athena and Hermes, with Zeus' permission. They had only obeyed their father's orders, and in any case, Aegyptus had told his sons to murder the girls as soon as possible so that he might claim the whole inheritance

Left: Centaur; *above:* Ixion on the wheel; *below:* Tityus and the vultures

The Danaids

which he disputed with Danaus. Despite this, however, the three Judges of the Dead found the girls guilty of a crime and sentenced them to be punished. They were given the endless task of filling a broken pot with water carried in sieves.

Things to do

Use the heading *Crime and Punishment*. Underline.

1 Describe in your own words the punishment of *three* of the following:

Tantalus; Sisyphus; Ixion; Tityus; the Danaids.

Be sure to mention why they were punished.

2 Draw three pictures to illustrate your answer to question 1. Colour each drawing.

3 Is there any reason why the Greeks should tell stories about such terrible punishments?

4 What feature did all these punishments have in common?

5 Devise a punishment (for someone who deserves it) that will have the same feature as those in the stories.

6 Finally, to refresh your memory about all the names concerned with The Land of the Dead, copy the short word-puzzle opposite into your notebook and try to do it.

Clues

Across

4 A barrier of water
5 A place of punishment
7 Sheer heaven!
8 Murderous wives
9 A monstrous dog
11 Three wild women
12 He cheated death
13 A wicked king who was sent spinning
14 He was angry with 12 across and rescued a god from him

Down

1 The reluctant queen
2 The old boatman
3 God of the Dead
5 He was always hungry and thirsty
6 He could not get to the top
10 Those who were punished have been guilty of——
11 Three wild women again!
14 A river god who was angry

51

11 Orpheus and Eurydice

One of the very few living mortals ever to enter the Land of the Dead, stealing past the fierce guard-dog Cerberus, and come back to earth again, was Orpheus.

Orpheus was the son of Oeagrus, King of Thrace and of Calliope, one of the nine Muses, the goddesses in charge of music, literature and art. She taught her son how to play the lyre and soon his music was so beautiful that wild beasts stopped, spellbound, to listen; birds stopped in their flight; fish leapt from the sea. Even trees and rocks moved to follow the sound of his music.

As a young man Orpheus travelled far and wide. He sailed with Jason and the Argonauts and his wonderful music helped the Argonauts overcome many of their difficulties in the quest for the Golden Fleece.

On his return home Orpheus met the wood-nymph Eurydice. He fell deeply in love with her—she was so beautiful and charming—and soon he married her. For a short time they were blissfully happy but something was about to happen that would change all that.

One day Eurydice was walking in the meadow near her home when Aristaeus, one of the countryside gods, attacked her.

Eurydice fled but Aristaeus ran after her. As she fled, Eurydice stepped on a snake which was lying hidden in the grass. The snake bit her on the ankle and Eurydice, overcome by the poison, fell to the ground dead.

Orpheus was grief-stricken. He longed to have his wife back again at his side. In desperation he decided to attempt the impossible—to go to the Land of the Dead and bring his wife back. His music charmed Charon, the old boatman, so much that he ferried Orpheus across the Styx free of charge. Even Cerberus, the three-headed dog who guarded the entrance, was lulled by the beauty of the music and let Orpheus pass into the Underworld. The three stern judges of the Dead, Aeacus, Rhadamanthys and Minos, looked kindly at this stranger in

Left to right: Orpheus; Orpheus meets Eurydice; Eurydice is attacked; Eurydice dies

their midst. As Orpheus went on his way, singing to the music of his lyre, the bloodless ghosts were in tears. All punishment ceased. Tantalus did not try to catch the fleeing waters; Ixion's wheel stood still in wonder; the vultures did not gnaw at Tityus' liver; the daughters of Danaus rested from their jars and Sisyphus sat still on his rock.

When at last he came to Hades himself, he played his music even more beautifully than before. His plea was simple and eloquent:

> I beg you, spin again the thread of Eurydice's life, brought too soon to its end. All that we humans have is owed to you and after waiting a little while, sooner or later, we all hurry here to this place. We are all on our way—this is our final home. She also, when she has completed the proper span of her years and is ready for death, will come within your power. I ask for her return as a gift from you; but if you refuse to give her back, I have made up my mind that I do not wish to return either: rejoice in the death of us both!

The gloomy God of Death, charmed by the music, agreed to Orpheus' request that Eurydice should be returned to the world above. He called Eurydice. She was among the ghosts who had newly come and she walked slowly as a result of her wound. Orpheus was overjoyed to see her, but Hades then told him of one condition: as he led her out of the Underworld, he must not look back at his wife until Eurydice had stepped out into the light of the sun. Orpheus gladly accepted this condition.

Off he went, still playing on the lyre, leading his wife up the steep path, through the deep silence, to the world above. They were not far from the surface when Orpheus, fearing that her strength might be failing and eager to see her, turned round. But it was too soon: Eurydice had not yet stepped out into the sunlight. Eurydice began to slip away. Stretching out his arm Orpheus strained to clasp her hands but he seized nothing but yielding air. Eurydice, dying now a second time, uttered no

Left to right: Orpheus pleads with Hades; Orpheus turns round too soon; he is heartbroken; the Maenads kill him

complaint but vanished into the darkness of the Underworld— this time forever.

Orpheus was completely heartbroken. No one could comfort him. If only he had not looked back his wife would still have been with him. He shut himself away, wishing to be alone in his bitter grief. He longed for death so that he could at last be reunited with his wife. Death would indeed come eventually —but in its own way. For Orpheus it came violently.

Orpheus, in his solitary state, refused to worship the new god Dionysus. He even complained that the new god set a bad example for men with his wild, drunken behaviour. In anger, Dionysus ordered the Maenads, the drunken young women who worshipped him, to attack Orpheus. They caught him off guard, without his magical lyre, and tore his body to pieces, throwing his head into the river Hebrus. It floated, still singing, down to the sea and was carried to the island of Lesbos.

The Muses collected all the other pieces of his body and buried them at the foot of Mount Olympus where now the nightingales sing more sweetly than anywhere else in Greece. Apollo, the god of music, took Orpheus' lyre and placed it in the sky as a constellation, still known to this day as The Lyre.

The Roman poet Ovid tells us that this sad story had a happy ending. Orpheus' ghost passed into the Underworld beneath the earth. He recognized all the places which he had seen before. He searched through the fields of Elysium until he found his wife Eurydice. He clasped her in his eager arms. There, in paradise, they walk side by side; or sometimes Orpheus follows as his wife walks in front; sometimes he leads the way and looks back, as he can do safely now, at his Eurydice.

Things to do

Section A

Write as the heading *Orpheus and Eurydice*.

1   Answer these questions in sentences:
    (a) What special power did Orpheus have?
    (b) Who was his wife?
    (c) How did she die?
    (d) How did Orpheus try to get her back? (Describe in detail).
    (e) What condition did he have to accept?
    (f) What happened when he broke the condition?
    (g) What did Orpheus do now?
    (h) Which god was angry with Orpheus and why?
    (i) How did Orpheus meet his death?
    (j) How does this story have a happy ending?
2   Choose any episode of this story that appeals to you. Draw a picture to illustrate the episode. Give your picture a title and colour it.

Section B

1   You are Orpheus and you have just lost your wife for the second time. Write a short essay, entitled 'If only . . .', to describe the sad events of your life.
2   Orpheus was not only a musician but also a fine poet. He might have written a poem in honour of his dead wife. The poem would have been beautiful but also very sad. Try to write a poem like this about the loss of Eurydice. Could you set your poem to music, making it into a song which Orpheus might have sung to the music of his lyre?
3   The god Dionysus was involved in the 'punishment' of another human—King Midas. Try to find a book in your school library which tells this story; write your own account of the story in your notebook and make a drawing to illustrate the story.

Part II
Stranger than Fiction?

1 Crete:
The Architect of
the Labyrinth

There are two popular stories in Greek mythology connected with the magnificent palace at Knossos on Crete, the largest of the Greek Islands.

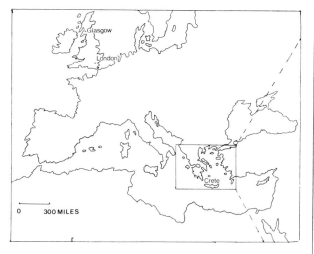

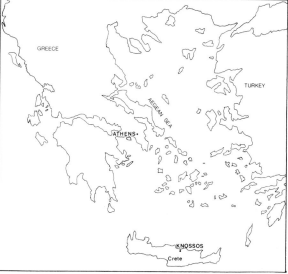

In the first story, Daedalus, an expert craftsman and inventor was expelled from his native city of Athens because he had grown jealous of his nephew Talus and killed him. Sadly Daedalus wandered all over the Mediterranean Sea from place to place with his son Icarus until finally he arrived at Crete where King Minos offered him the hospitality of his palace at Knossos. Both Daedalus and Icarus lived happily at Knossos, but soon they suffered the king's anger. When the king's wife gave birth to the Minotaur—a terrible creature which was half man and half bull—Minos was convinced that Daedalus was involved in this outrage. He forced Daedalus to build a

An ant threading a shell

The lament of Icarus

Labyrinth, a maze constructed in such a way that the Minotaur would be totally unable to escape. When the Labyrinth was completed, Minos locked Daedalus and his son Icarus inside it.

Minos' wife helped them to escape from the Labyrinth, but despite this they could not escape from the island because the harbours were so well guarded. Any hope of escape seemed impossible. Daedalus, however, did not despair. He constructed two huge pairs of wings, made out of wax and covered with feathers. The smaller pair he gave to his son Icarus with these instructions:

'My son, be on your guard! Don't fly too high because the sun will melt the wax, and don't fly too low, for the sea will wet the feathers.'

Putting on their wings, father and son flew off. Soon, unfortunately, Icarus became so delighted with the power of the wings that he forgot what his father had told him, and flew higher and higher. Disaster! The sun melted the wax and helplessly Icarus plunged headlong into the sea to his death.

After burying his son, Daedalus flew on to Sicily where the king was pleased to receive him. Daedalus made numerous toys for the king's children. In the meantime, King Minos was so furious with Daedalus' escape, that he determined to pursue and kill him.

When he arrived at Sicily, Minos asked the king if he knew anyone who could thread a very complicated shell which he had, for he knew that Daedalus would be the only person who could do this. The king gave the shell to Daedalus who was quick to solve the problem.

He attached a piece of thread to an ant. Next he bored a hole at the point of the shell and attracted the ant to go through the shell by smearing honey at the other end.

Immediately Minos demanded that Daedalus be handed over to him. The king's daughters, however, who had become very fond of Daedalus decided to save him by killing Minos. They had a pipe installed over the bathtub which Minos used. Some time later when Minos was taking a bath, they poured boiling water through the pipe and Minos was instantly killed. Daedalus left Sicily, however, for his own protection and settled safely in Sardinia where he continued to invent new machines until he died.

Things to do

Section A

Write down in your notebook and underline the following:
Crete: Daedalus and Icarus. Answer the following questions:
1 Which is the largest of the Greek islands?
2 What famous building was there at Knossos?
3 Who was Daedalus? Where did he come from? What was the name of his son?
4 Who was the king at the palace of Knossos?
5 Why was the king angry with Daedalus?
6 What did the king force Daedalus to build?
7 What did he do after it was completed?
8 When Daedalus was imprisoned, who helped him to escape?
9 Why was it still impossible to escape from the island?
10 What did Daedalus invent?
11 What instructions did he give to Icarus?
12 What caused Icarus' death?
13 Write a short account of what happened to Daedalus after he arrived at the island of Sicily.

Section B

1 Draw and paint a picture of the Minotaur.
2 Try to construct a Labyrinth or maze. Mark a point within it with an X, and ask one of your friends to find his way out of it.
3 Draw a picture of the ant threading the shell.
4 Design a medallion commemorating the history of flight with Daedalus and Icarus on it.
5 Man has always wanted to fly under his own power, e.g.

Left: A wing designed by Leonardo da Vinci

Below: Hang gliding

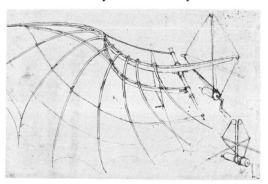

Try to find some more illustrations like these and put them in your notebook.

2 Crete: The Monster of the Labyrinth

There is another frightening story connected with the island of Crete. Minos, the King of Crete, had sent his son Androgeus to visit Aegeus, King of Athens. Near Athens there was a fierce bull which no warrior had been able to kill. It was huge and terrifying. Foolishly, Androgeus determined to test his skill against this bull. He was no match for it and was killed. When King Minos heard that his son had been killed, he was so furious with Aegeus and the Athenians, that he invaded and destroyed all the land around Athens. He was not content with this punishment alone. Every year from then onwards, the people of Athens were to send to Crete an offering of seven girls and seven boys. A cruel and horrible death awaited them, for they were thrown into the Labyrinth of the Minotaur—the creature that was half bull and half man—who ate them alive.

When Theseus grew up, hatred for Minos and the Minotaur increased within him. He asked his father, King Aegeus, 'Is the Minotaur very big and fierce?'

'The Minotaur,' said his father Aegeus, 'lives inside a huge Labyrinth of stone which the architect Daedalus built for King Minos. It has many winding passages, and if anyone enters it, he will be lost because it is impossible to find the way out again. Even the Minotaur himself cannot escape from it and he moves about looking for human beings to devour.'

Theseus immediately decided to do something to put an end to this wickedness. He volunteered as one of the seven boys, when the time for the next sacrifice came around. Aegeus naturally was very worried and upset, because he wanted Theseus to be king after he died.

'Don't worry, father,' said Theseus, 'I will slay the Minotaur and come back home.' Aegeus could not prevent his son sailing away with the others to Crete. As Theseus was leaving the following day, his father said to him tearfully, 'I shall watch every day for your safe return to Athens. When you return, remember to haul down these black sails which indicate death and hoist white sails in their place. In this way I shall know that you are safe.' Theseus agreed and set sail.

When the Athenian ship arrived at Crete, they were taken to the palace at Knossos where King Minos was feasting at a banquet. After telling them that they would all die the following day at the hands of the Minotaur, he had them thrown into prison. Minos' daughter, however, the princess Ariadne, had fallen in love with Theseus as soon as she had seen him, and she decided to help him. Secretly she had obtained the key to the prison, and crept close to the couch where Theseus was sleeping and whispered to him, 'Theseus you must not die. Take this sword and hide it under your cloak. Here is a ball of string. Take it when you enter the Labyrinth. Tie it to a rock and unroll it as you proceed. You will thus be able to find your way out again by following the string back to the entrance.'

'Who are you?' enquired Theseus.

'My name is Ariadne', she replied, 'and I am the daughter of King Minos.'

'What is your reason for helping me like this?' asked Theseus.

'Aphrodite, the goddess of love', replied Ariadne, 'has asked me to do this and in return for my help you must promise to marry me.'

Theseus then promised to marry her if he slew the Minotaur.

The next day when the seven boys and seven girls were thrown into the Labyrinth. Theseus turned round and told the rest to stay where they were because he wanted to approach the Minotaur alone.

On and on down the endless passages of the Labyrinth walked Theseus unwinding the string as he proceeded. The stone walls were damp and ice-cold. His heart was beating loudly as now and again he stopped to look for signs of the Minotaur lying in one of the passages in a deep sleep. Roused from its sleep, it let out such a tremendous bellow that the walls rattled and shook.

The creature scrambled to its feet, lowered its head with fire pouring out of its nostrils and charged at Theseus. He caught hold of one of its horns with his left hand, pulled its head back and plunged his sword into its neck. The beast let out a terrible groan, slumped forward and fell to the ground dead.

Theseus retraced his way to the entrance where he met his friends who were overjoyed to see him alive.

'We will have to stay here till night' said Theseus 'so that the guards will believe that we are all dead. Then Ariadne will open the door of the Labyrinth and let us out.'

Night came. Ariadne unlocked the door and hurried with

Theseus sets sail for Crete

Theseus enters the labyrinth

Theseus kills the Minotaur

Theseus and his friends to the ship that was waiting ready for them at the harbour. Quietly they sailed away. So that Minos could not pursue them, they had made holes in his ships and sunk them. Happily they sailed away to the open sea.

Luck, however, was not on the side of Ariadne. Soon a storm arose and they were forced to shelter on the island of Naxos. While they were sleeping at night Dionysus, the god of wine, appeared and touched the brows of the Athenians to wipe away any memory of Ariadne for he wanted her to be his wife.

The next day Theseus and his friends woke early and sailed away leaving poor Ariadne behind. Theseus sat moodily alone at the bow of the ship. The ship was gradually nearing Athens and still Theseus remained silent and deep in thought. Calamity! He had forgotten to take down the black sails and hoist the white ones. Aegeus who had stood every day on the cliff top and waited anxiously for his son's return, saw the dark sails appearing on the horizon. The pain of despair was too much for him and he tossed himself headlong into the sea to his death. The next day Theseus buried his father in a hero's tomb and named the sea where his father had died the 'Aegean Sea' so that he would not be forgotten. Theseus became King of Athens, united all the people in the villages around Athens into the single state later called Attica and it was as a result of this unification that Athens grew stronger and stronger to form an empire.

Things to do

Section A

Write down in your notebook and underline the following: *Crete: Theseus and the Minotaur.* Answer the following questions:
1   Who was the King of Athens?
2   How was Theseus related to the king?
3   Why was Minos so furious with the Athenians?
4   What did Minos do to the land around Athens?
5   What cruel punishment did he impose on the Athenian people?
6   Who built the Labyrinth?
7   What did Theseus volunteer to do?
8   What did Aegeus ask Theseus to do if he returned home safely?
9   Who helped Theseus escape from the Labyrinth. How did she do this? Why did she do this?
10   Describe in your own words all that happened after Ariadne left Crete with Theseus and his companions.

Section B

1   Draw a picture of Theseus killing the Minotaur.
2   Draw a strip cartoon telling the story of Theseus' journey home from Crete to Athens.
3   Try to compose a song about the story of Theseus and the Minotaur to the music of some well-known tune.

3 Crete:
True or False?

These two stories—Daedalus and Icarus, Theseus and the Minotaur have never ceased to fascinate people over many hundreds of years with their colour and imagery. The pictures of a magnificent palace, a huge labyrinth and a terrible creature that is half bull and half man, are certainly attractive. Sir Arthur John Evans, the British archaeologist, was convinced that there might have been more to these stories.

He began his excavations at Knossos in 1900 and continued them until 1935 when he left Crete at the age of 84. Working with great patience and determination, he was able to rediscover the glorious civilization which flourished in Crete about 1700–1450 BC. He excavated the beautiful palace at Knossos where King Minos is supposed to have lived.

Sir Arthur Evans

The palace of Knossos

It is estimated that the palace covered an area of 22 000 square metres and that about 100 000 people lived in and around the palace. This was a vast area for a palace and a very large population to support.

The palace is thought to have contained 1500 rooms, and so it is not surprising to see where the story of a maze or labyrinth originated.

The main part of the building was the central court which was used for religious services. Where did the idea of the Minotaur come from? The bull was sacred and important to the Cretans because it fertilized the herd which was so necessary to them for meat and milk. They identified it with the heavens and the sun which make the earth productive with rain and heat. Furthermore, the island of Crete has always been liable to earthquakes. Indeed, Sir Arthur Evans wrote in his notebook when he was excavating that there was an earthquake which sounded like the roars of an angry bull. The Cretans had many paintings of scenes with bulls in them and like the Spaniards of today, young Cretans could prove their courage by risking their lives against a bull.

Bull-leaping

The young athletes gripped the bull's horns, somersaulted over its back and landed on its rump. Spectacles such as this would take place in the central courtyard.

It is clear that the palace itself must have been a very busy place. It contained rooms set aside for storage and manufacturing.

Cretan jars in storeroom

Each of these jars could hold 29 gallons of oil, and there was storage space for 420 such jars. This means that 12 000 gallons of oil could be stored at any time. Most of this was exported together with wine, cypress wood and woven cloth which could be dyed with purple obtained from the shellfish, known as murex, easily found near the Cretan shore. Crete was a place of tremendous commercial activity, trading with all parts of the Mediterranean. The map below illustrates the extent of the trading in which she was involved.

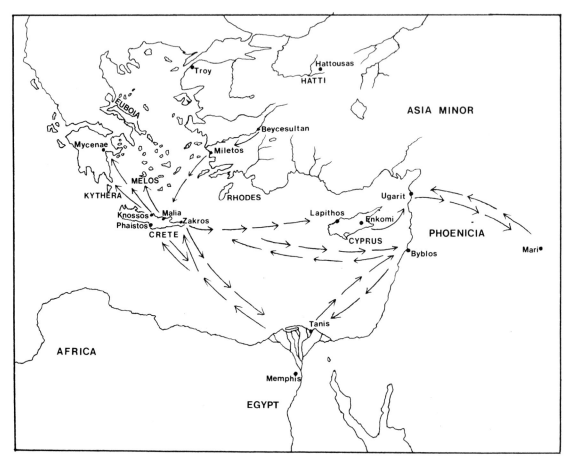

Cretan trade routes

This trading led to a high standard of living for the people of Crete who passed on their advances in art and craftsmanship to people all over the Mediterranean. The island of Thera (Santorine) which lies quite near Crete enjoyed much of the benefits of the Cretan way of life until about 1450 BC when there was a catastrophic earthquake which wiped out almost the whole island and must have produced terrible damage to Crete and other islands with its tidal wave. At any rate, the power of Crete began to subside around this time.

The volcano of Thera erupting in 1926

Things to do

Section A

Write down in your notebook and underline the following: *Life and Buildings in Ancient Crete.* Answer the following questions:
1 Who excavated the palace at Knossos?
2 How long did his excavations last?
3 What does the word 'Labyrinth' mean?
4 Where did the idea of the Minotaur come from?
5 How could young Cretans prove their courage?
6 What were the main articles of trade for the Cretans?
7 Why did Crete cease to be such an important centre in the Mediterranean?

Section B

1 Draw or trace the map showing the places in the Mediterranean with which Crete traded.
2 Here is a stamp issued by the Post Office commemorating some important occasion. Design a similar postage stamp for Ancient Crete.

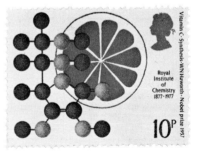

4 Troy:
To War for
a Woman

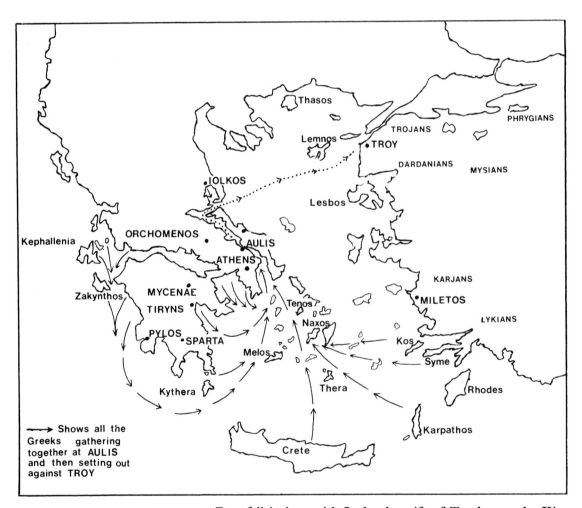

The Trojan war expedition

Shows all the Greeks gathering together at AULIS and then setting out against TROY

Zeus fell in love with Leda, the wife of Tyndareus, the King of Sparta. He appeared to Leda in the form of a swan and afterwards Leda produced an egg from which was born a girl who was given the name of Helen. She was no ordinary girl. Indeed, she grew up to be so beautiful that many princes from all over Greece flocked to Sparta with the hope of marrying her. Tyndareus was at a loss as to whom he should allow to marry Helen, because he was afraid that the unsuccessful princes would make war on the favoured one. Before making a choice, therefore, Tyndareus made all the princes take an oath that they would protect the marriage of the one who won Helen. Then he chose Menelaus and gave his kingdom to him. Menelaus and Helen soon had a daughter, Hermione, and lived happily together. Their happiness, however, was short-lived because events were happening elsewhere destined to bring disaster to their marriage. How did this happen?

While the gods one day were celebrating a feast, Eris, the goddess of quarrelling and fighting, suddenly appeared and threw down a golden apple with the words 'For the most beautiful goddess' inscribed on it. Immediately all the goddesses began to quarrel, each claiming the apple as hers. Eventually three goddesses only were left in the contest—Hera, queen of the gods, Athena, goddess of wisdom, and Aphrodite, goddess of love. Zeus intervened and said: 'Hermes, the messenger of the gods, will escort you to Mount Ida where Paris, the son of Priam, king of Troy, will decide the winner of this beauty contest.'

Hermes led the three goddesses to Mount Ida where they found Paris, resting on the hillside playing sweet music and his herdsman's crook lying beside him. Paris was startled, but Hermes calmed and reassured him: 'Don't be afraid, Paris. I have been sent by Zeus who knows that you have always been fair when judging anything. I have three goddesses here with me and you must decide, by the command of Zeus, which of the three is the most beautiful.' Paris was afraid, for he knew that if he chose one of them, he would anger the other two.

Hera was first to approach him. 'If you choose me,' she said with authority, 'I will give you as much land in Asia as you wish and make you more powerful than any other king.' Paris did not know what to say, so overpowered was he in her presence. As he looked again, he came face to face with Athena whose brilliant eyes and shining helmet dazzled him. 'You will be the wisest of men,' said Athena, 'if you choose me, and with wisdom there will be no end to the lands you will conquer.' Such promises of fame and power made Paris wonder and for a moment he began to day-dream of what might happen to him. Suddenly he became aware of Aphrodite, the goddess of love, being near to him. His eyes were riveted as he beheld her beauty.

Paris judging the beauty contest

Aphrodite spoke to Paris in her soft and persuasive voice. 'Forget about the promises of these others, my dear Paris, for they will only involve you in the evils of war. No, choose me and you choose love. I will give you the most beautiful woman in the world, Helen of Sparta, and she will be yours.' Paris could not resist and was completely overpowered by her smile. Without hesitation he handed over to her the golden apple and Aphrodite was the winner of the beauty contest. Aphrodite was pleased with her success and turned to Paris. 'Well, Paris,' she said, 'I will always be at your side to help you now, and with my help you shall have beautiful Helen.'

Paris said farewell to his father, Priam, King of Troy, and his mother Hecuba and sailed away to Greece. When Menelaus received news that Paris was coming to visit Sparta, he assembled all his nobles to welcome him.

'Noble Paris,' said Menelaus as he greeted him, 'you are welcome in my palace and I hope you enjoy your visit,' When Paris saw Helen, he was immediately struck by her beauty, and Helen felt quite uneasy in his presence. As the days passed this attraction became stronger and stronger. One evening Menelaus told him that he might have to go away for a while. 'My friend

Idomeneus of Crete has invited me,' said Menelaus, 'to join him in a hunting expedition. I hope that you will not be annoyed, Paris, because I have to go away for some time. Helen, my dear wife, will look after you until I return.'

After Menelaus departed Helen and Paris were alone. Paris told her of the beauty contest among the goddesses. 'I love you, Helen,' he said, 'and I could not keep my secret from you any longer.' The goddess Aphrodite had visited Helen and made her fall in love with Paris. Paris took hold of her hand and quietly they left the palace and sailed away to Troy.

Paris and Helen secretly run away

News of the elopement soon spread throughout Greece and all the islands. Messengers were sent to Paris demanding at once that Helen be given back to her husband Menelaus. This was refused, for even old Priam, King of Troy, was won over by the charm and beauty of Helen. Menelaus and his brother Agamemnon, King of Mycenae, gathered together the princes who had come to marry Helen and reminded them of their oath to protect the marriage of the one who won Helen as a wife. They were determined to bring Helen back to Menelaus. Achilles, Diomedes, Ajax and Odysseus and many other famous warriors helped Menelaus and Agamemnon to assemble a fleet of 1000 ships. A terrible war was about to begin.

Things to do

Section A

Write down in your notebook and underline the following:
The Trojan War: The Cause of the War. Answer the following
questions:
1 Which Greek city did Tyndareus rule?
2 What was Tyndareus' wife called?
3 How was Helen born?
4 What was Helen famous for?
5 Who married Helen?
6 What oath did Tyndareus force upon the princes who
   wanted to marry Helen?
7 Who was the goddess Eris?
8 Which three goddesses took part in a beauty contest?
9 What was the prize for the most beautiful goddess?
10 Who won the beauty contest?
11 What did this goddess promise to Paris?
12 What happened when Paris ran away with Helen?

Section B

1 Draw a picture of Helen.
2 If you had a choice of being very powerful or very wise or
   very beautiful, which would you choose? Give some reasons
   for your choice.
3 Act the scene where Paris runs away with Helen and what
   happens after this is discovered.

5 Troy: Achilles and Hector

The Greek ships sailed across the Aegean Sea and landed on the coast of Asia Minor near the city of Troy. After making sure that their ships were safely at anchor they quickly built their camp, prepared to stay for as long as it took to regain Helen and punish the Trojans. The first few days were very busy for the Greeks. Soon their huts and tents were dotted all along the shore. Beyond this there stretched an open plain and further inland there was the city of Troy built on a high hill. Surrounding and protecting the city was a huge strong wall and it seemed impossible to capture it. Nothing, however, could stop the Greeks.

From time to time the Trojans rushed out from their city to attack the Greeks and most of this fighting took place in the plain between the city and the shore. The Greeks made no attempt on their part to storm the wall and enter the city. They were content to wait for the Trojans to come out and then attack. The war stumbled on in this way for nine long years with neither side gaining complete victory. The Greek soldiers by this time saw little prospect of recovering Helen and grew more and more dissatisfied. Even their leaders began to quarrel. Achilles, the greatest of the Greek warriors, refused to fight any more because Agamemnon took away from him a Trojan slave girl. Without Achilles, the Greek soldiers lost heart with the result that the Trojans drove them right back to the sea and burned some of their ships. Still Achilles refused to help. Patroclus, his closest friend, went alone to Achilles who sat brooding in his hut.

'Achilles, my friend,' said Patroclus imploringly, 'we are not doing well in the battle. Even now the Trojans are attacking our ships. Agamemnon, Odysseus and many others are wounded.'

'What do you want me to do?' said Achilles.

'I know that you will not fight yourself, Achilles,' said Patroclus, 'but if you give me your armour which strikes terror into the Trojans, then I will pretend to be you and I am sure that

Fighting before the walls of Troy

with this I will be able to drive back the enemy.'

'Take my armour and chariot if you wish,' muttered Achilles, softening for the first time, 'and tell my men to follow you.'

As soon as the Trojans saw the chariot and the armour they started to retreat. The gods, however, decided to intervene. Zeus sent Apollo to help the Trojans and he knocked off the helmet from the head of Patroclus. When Hector noticed this he turned round and wounded Patroclus with a spear so that he fell to the ground seriously wounded.

'Patroclus,' shouted Hector in triumph, 'you boasted that you would capture my city and take away our women to your ships as slaves. Fool, that you are! You are about to die and the vultures will devour you.'

Hector put his foot on the dead Patroclus, pulled out his spear and then took away the armour from him.

When Achilles heard what had happened he wept and then became angry. He vowed to avenge his friend's death.

Achilles' mother, Thetis, the sea-goddess heard him sighing and moaning. She hurried to Hephaestus, the God of fire, and asked him to make Achilles a new suit of armour which she brought to him while he was asleep. The next morning Achilles put this on with one thought in his mind—to kill Hector.

When Hector came out of the city and saw the polished armour of Achilles gleaming in the sun he ran off in a panic. Achilles chased him like a hawk after a dove. After they ran three times round the walls of the city the goddess Athena decided to intervene and help Achilles. She took on the appearance of Deiphobus, Hector's brother, and approached Hector.

'Why are you running away like this?' she said. 'Let the two of us stand and fight him together.'

Hector stopped and prepared to fight. He shouted defiantly to Achilles, 'You have made me run, but I will meet you now and you will die.'

There was anger in Achilles' eyes as he said, 'You will pay with your life for the death of my dear friend Patroclus and the wounds that you inflicted on my comrades. There will be no more talk, your end is near.'

He threw his long spear which Hector side-stepped and it stuck deep into the ground. Athena secretly picked it up and gave it back to him. Next, Hector threw his spear, but it struck Achilles' shield and rebounded. Hector turned round to call his brother Deiphobus and saw nobody there. His courage fell.

'I have been tricked by Athena,' he moaned, 'and I thought Deiphobus was by my side; I cannot escape death now.'

He drew out his sharp sword and pounced at Achilles who protected himself with his splendid shield and his spear flashing

74

high into the air. Achilles aimed his spear at Hector's collar bone just where it joins the neck and Hector dropped to the ground with a tremendous thump.

'Hector, you have now paid for the death of my dear friend,' roared Achilles, 'and I will now fling you to the dogs.'

Achilles removed Hector's armour and slit the tendons of his feet from ankle to heel. Then he passed thongs of leather through them and tied this to his chariot-wheels. He put the armour on the chariot, mounted, and lashed his horses. The body of Hector was dragged along the ground, with his head trailing in the dust.

Achilles did not allow Hector to be given a funeral, but celebrated Patroclus' funeral with athletic contests which were usual for the occasion. There was chariot-racing, boxing, armed fighting and javelin throwing. The Trojans begged Achilles to return the body of Hector for burial but still he refused. Zeus, however, persuaded Achilles to hand over the body and sent Hermes to escort Priam through the Greek army to Achilles. At last Hector's body was returned and he was given a decent funeral. Not long after this, Achilles was accidentally killed by a poisoned arrow, shot by Paris, which pierced his heel. This was the only part of his body which was vulnerable. Thetis, his mother, had dipped him when he was a baby in the river Styx in the underworld, to protect him against wounds. However, she had held him by the ankle to prevent him being carried away by the strong current. His heel, therefore, remained out of the water and so was unprotected. Paris himself was killed in a contest with a Greek archer, and Helen was married to his brother Deiphobus, another of Priam's sons. It was quite apparent to the Greeks that Troy could not be captured by force. Something else would have to be done.

Things to do

Section A

Write down in your notebook and underline the following:
The Fighting at Troy. Answer these questions:
  1 Which sea did the Greeks sail across to reach Troy?
  2 What did the Greeks do first of all, when they reached Troy?
  3 What did the city of Troy look like?
  4 Where and for how long did most of the fighting take place?
  5 Why did Achilles refuse to fight any more?
  6 How did Patroclus die?
  7 What did Hector do when he saw Achilles?
  8 Which goddess tricked Hector?
  9 How did Achilles treat Hector's body after he killed him?
 10 How did Achilles celebrate Patroclus' funeral?
 11 Which god helped Priam to recover Hector's body?
 12 How did Achilles die?

Section B

 1 Make a drawing showing the scene of the fighting around Troy as you imagine it would have been.
 2 Read the following piece of poetry about Achilles and Hector:

Fierce, at the word, his weighty sword he drew,
And, all collected, on Achilles flew.
So Jove's bold bird, high balanced in the air.
Stoops from the clouds to truss the quivering hare.
Nor less Achilles his fierce soul prepares:
Before his breast the flaming shield he bears
Refulgent orb! above his fourfold cone
The gilded horse-hair sparkled in the sun
Nodding at every step: (Vulcanian frame!)
And as he moved, his figure seem'd on flame.
As radiant Hesper shines with keener light
Far-beaming o'er the silver host of night
When all the starry train emblaze the sphere:
So shone the point of great Achilles' spear.
In his right hand he waves the weapon round,
Eyes the whole man, and meditates the wound;
But the rich mail Patroclus lately wore
Securely cased the warrior's body o'er.
One space at length he spies, to let in fate

Where 'twixt the neck and throat the jointed plate
Gave entrance: through that penetrable part
Furious he drove the well-directed dart:
Nor pierced the windpipe yet, nor took the power
Of speech, unhappy! from thy dying hour.
Prone on the field the bleeding warrior lies,
While, thus triumphing, stern Achilles cries:

These are a few lines of Alexander Pope's translation of
Homer's *Iliad*, which tells the story of the Trojan war. The
lines are taken from the part where Achilles kills Hector.
Try to write a piece of poetry about another scene from the
fighting at Troy.

3 Imagine yourself as an ordinary Greek soldier or Trojan
woman during all this fighting. Describe your feelings.

6 Troy: The Death of a City

It was now the tenth year of the war and the Greeks were very dispirited. The city of Troy still stood intact, her solid walls offering her protection against the Greeks. Odysseus who was the cleverest and most cunning of the Greeks, realized that something else would have to be done and very soon, because the Greek soldiers were beginning to quarrel too often and many of them wanted to go back home and abandon the war.

'I must work out some other way of getting into Troy,' thought Odysseus to himself, 'because we are just wasting our time trying to attack it.'

As soon as he had devised his plan, Odysseus asked Agamemnon to call together the other Greek princes.

'I have a plan,' said Odysseus. 'This is what I suggest that we do. We'll build a huge wooden horse and leave the inside of its belly hollow and empty. This part we can cram full of our best warriors. After doing this we'll leave it on the open plain and with the rest of our army on board their ships we'll pretend to sail away to Greece, but really only to the island of Tenedos just off the coast. There we'll stay until we receive the signal to come back and attack Troy. While we are sailing back, Sinon, this slave here, will allow himself to be captured. He'll convince the Trojans that the wooden horse was built by us as an offering to the goddess Athena for our safe journey home. He'll explain to them that if they take it inside Troy, Athena will then protect them and she will turn her anger on the Greeks. After the horse is inside Troy, we can kill off the guards and open the gates to let in the rest of our soldiers.'

The plan was immediately accepted by the rest of the princes and during the following weeks there was great activity in the Greek camp. First they constructed a sky-scraper of a horse. Then they dismantled the camp and put their stores on their ships. When all this was done the best Greek warriors with Odysseus as their leader were secretly concealed inside the horse. The rope-ladder was hauled up and the trap door shut.

That night the rest of the Greeks sailed away. The next morning the Trojans woke up. They were amazed to see that after such a long time the Greeks had finally departed. They opened the gates and streamed out to have a look at the derelict positions of the Greeks on the shore. Then they gaped at the tremendous bulk of the horse.

What were they to do with it? Should they break it down and throw it into the sea because the Greeks were never to be trusted?

Should they believe that it might be an offering to the goddess Athena and take it into their city? While they were arguing about these suggestions, the priest Laocoon came tearing out of the city.

'My fellow Trojans,' he shouted in great temper. 'Are you all stark mad? Do you really believe our foes are gone? Do you imagine any Greek gift is guileless? Is that your idea of Ulysses (Odysseus)? This thing of wood conceals Greek soldiers, or else it is a mechanism designed against our walls —to pry into our homes and to bear down on the city; sure, some trick is there. No, you must never feel safe with the horse, Trojans. Whatever it is, I distrust the Greeks, even when they are generous.' (*Aeneid* of Virgil, translated by C. Day Lewis.)

With these words said, he grasped a heavy spear and hurled it with all his might. The spear stuck quivering in the belly of the horse so that its hollow inside resounded and grumbled. Laocoon was leading the others to destroy the horse when suddenly some Trojan shepherds dragged in the Greek slave Sinon.

'Who are you?' they said. 'Tell us the truth and exactly all that you know or else we shall kill you instantly.'

'My name is Sinon,' he said, 'and although I am a Greek, I hate the Greeks because they treated me badly and they were going to kill me. Yes, you can be sure that the Greeks are gone and I never want to see any of them again.'

'Why then have they gone and why did they want to kill you?' they asked Sinon.

'They campaigned here too long,' replied Sinon, 'and if Agamemnon had not agreed to sail back home, there would have been a mutiny. They wanted to sacrifice me to the gods for their safe return but I broke out of prison and lay all night concealed in the mud of a lake among the reeds and waited for them to sail away to Greece where I can never more see my father or my little sons. This wooden horse which you see here was built to Athena and the Greeks built it so high that it could not be taken through the gates of Troy and become your protector.'

The Trojans felt pity for Sinon. 'Untie his hands,' ordered King Priam, and he spoke to Sinon in a friendly tone. 'Whoever you are, from now on forget about the Greeks. You are now one of us.'

Meanwhile something terrible happened to Laocoon who had gone to sacrifice a bull to Poseidon near the seashore. While he was performing the sacrifice with the help of his two sons, there appeared on the calm sea two sea-snakes—and they were making for the shore. They hissed and slithered out of the water on to the dry sand with their tongues flickering and a terrible bloodshot look in their eyes. Tightly round the bodies of Laocoon's sons they wound their coils and sank their fangs into their flesh. Laocoon hurried to help them with his sword in his hand and lashed out at the snakes. They wound themselves round him and squashed him to death while his cries echoed all around. After this they disappeared to the shrine of Athena inside Troy.

The Trojans believed that Laocoon had committed a crime by throwing the spear and now was being punished for his crime.

'The gods have been angry,' they shouted. 'We must take the wooden horse inside our city.' So they pulled down a part of the great wall of Troy, put rollers under the horse's hooves and ropes round its neck and straining all together they pulled its massive bulk inside the city. That night there was dancing and feasting to celebrate the end of the war. Meanwhile under cover of darkness, the Greek army had sailed back from the island of Tenedos and were waiting for the signal to attack.

When most of the Trojans had fallen asleep, tired out by dancing and overcome by too much wine, Sinon crept up to the horse and opened the secret trap door. Odysseus and his men slid down their rope ladder. Quietly they moved through the Trojans lying in their drunken sleep, killed the sentries at the gates, allowing the rest of the Greek soldiers inside the city. Within minutes Troy was burning in flames and almost all of its people were slaughtered. Helen was finally returned to her husband Menelaus. The war was over and they sailed back to Greece.

Things to do

Section A

Write down in your notebook and underline the following: *The Capture of Troy*. Write the following paragraph into your notebook filling in the blanks:

The cleverest of the Greeks was . . . . . . who worked out a plan for capturing Troy. He suggested that the Greeks should build a . . . . . . and leave the inside of its belly . . . . . . and . . . . . . They would fill it with their best . . . . . . and leave it on the open . . . . . . The rest of the Greeks then would sail away to the island . . . . They would stay there until they received the signal from the slave . . . . . . and they would return and capture . . . . When the Trojans woke up and saw the wooden horse, many wanted to bring it . . . . . . their city. Laocoon, however, advised them that it was a . . . . . . He grasped a heavy . . . . . . and hurled it at the horse. The Trojans decided to take the horse inside the city after they heard the story which . . . . . . told them. Laocoon was punished for throwing the spear at the horse. Two . . . . . . came out of the sea and . . . . . . him. That night there was . . . . . . and . . . . to celebrate the end of the war. When the Trojans had fallen asleep, ... and his men slid down the ladder and . . . . . . the sentries. The rest of the Greeks entered the . . . . . . Within minutes almost all of the Trojans were . . . .

Section B

1 Make a drawing of Laocoon being killed by the sea-snakes.
2 Imagine yourself as a Trojan at the feast after the horse had been taken into the city. Compose a song to celebrate the end of the war.
3 Act the scene where the Trojans waken up to find the wooden horse outside their city, and what follows.

Laocoon and his sons being killed by the serpents

7 Troy: Schliemann's Dream

Homer

The Greeks looked back with pride at the Trojan war. It was a great national victory for them and they were moved by the heroism of their ancestors. It was this which inspired Homer, who lived about 850 BC, to compose the *Iliad*, one of the finest poems that was ever written, about the episodes of the Trojan war.

For centuries his poem was recited by travelling minstrels at Greek banquets and it became the Bible for them in all questions of behaviour, law, politics and science. Yet, did the Trojan war really happen or was it just a story that was invented? The Greeks themselves believed that it did take place.

Thucydides, the Greek historian, writes:

There seems to have been no unity of the Greeks in war before the Trojan war. Because they lived separated in independent states, they never united in any great enterprise before the Trojan war. They made the expedition against Troy only after they had gained considerable experience of the sea.

This belief in the fact that the Trojan war was a real event in history became something that was passed on throughout the centuries and the thrilling episodes in Homer's *Iliad* kept the belief alive. If the story of the Trojan war was true, were Troy and Mycenae real places that actually existed? One person who was fully convinced was Heinrich Schliemann.

Right from his childhood when he first heard the exciting stories in Homer's *Iliad*, Schliemann had dreamed of bringing Homer's world to life again by discovering the sites of the placed mentioned in the *Iliad*. Schliemann was so determined that late in life he learned both ancient and modern Greek and took up the study of archaeology. This determination led him to discover in 1870 the site of Ancient Troy which he excavated. He was able to prove that a large and very ancient city had been continuously occupied from about 3000 BC.

Schliemann discovered that Troy had been destroyed nine times probably by fire and each time a new city was built over the old one. It was the seventh city of Troy, which he calculated to have been burned to the ground about 1250 BC, that figured in the *Iliad* of Homer. Many remains were discovered. Bones of horses were found. There was a considerable amount of Greek pottery suggesting regular trading with Greece. Many clay loom-weights found in the houses indicate that weaving was very common, particularly weaving of woollen garments as would appear from the large collection of bones of sheep and goats. Huge jars were also unearthed which could store large quantities of food and water.

His successful discovery of Troy encouraged Schliemann to search for Mycenae, the home of Agamemnon who led the Greeks against the Trojans. Again his efforts were worthwhile. In 1876 he discovered Mycenae when he excavated the circle of graves which is behind the 'Lion Gate' in the illustration below.

Heinrich Schliemann

The Lion Gate, Mycenae

A gold disc

These graves contained a large quantity of treasure which revealed the existence of a very advanced civilization. Nineteen bodies, including the bodies of two infants had been buried in the circle of graves. The bodies were most likely, judging from the treasure, those of members of the royal family.

The gold diadem, gold death masks, gold brooch, gold rings, and gold discs, all show us that the people who lived at Mycenae were very rich and prosperous.

Two women from Mycenae looking after a child

Warriors from Mycenae

The size, variety and excellence of the weapons in the tombs indicate that the Mycenaeans were a warlike people, just the sort of vigorous Greeks who could have attacked Troy. The evidence seems to show that there really was a great war between the Greeks and the Trojans. However, it is not absolutely certain what caused the war. Was the abduction of Helen the cause of the war? This was probably a romantic invention by Homer. A more reasonable explanation would seem to have been jealousy and disagreement over trade.

Geographically, the location of Troy was very important. It controlled the entrance to the Black Sea and the surrounding lands. The Greeks, who were greatly interested in trading around this area, probably attempted a large scale expedition to Troy with the intention of establishing themselves firmly on the coast. This naturally clashed with the interests of the Trojans who vigorously resisted their invasion; but the romantic version given by Homer was more attractive for his poem.

84

Things to do

Section A

Write down in your notebook and underline the following:
Troy and Mycenae. Answer the following questions:
1 What is the name of the Greek poet who wrote about the Trojan war?
2 What is the name of the poem he wrote which tells us about the Trojan War?
3 Where did the travelling minstrels recite this poem?
4 Why was the poem important to the Greeks?
5 Who excavated Troy and Mycenae?
6 How many cities of Troy were there?
7 When did the Trojan war take place?
8 What is the most reasonable explanation for the cause of the Trojan War?

Section B

1 If you were going to excavate a site, what equipment do you think you would require?
2 Should a person who discovers something old and precious be allowed to keep it? Discuss.
3 Make a drawing of some of the precious things found in the graves.

Part III
Travellers'
Tales

1 A Warrior Returns

Odysseus was the king of Ithaca, an island off the western coast of Greece. He had gone to Troy with the Greeks and had fought bravely there for ten years. He had, in fact, been responsible for the destruction of the city for it was he who had thought of the idea of the wooden horse.

After Troy fell, Odysseus wanted only to return to his homeland and his wife Penelope and son Telemachus.

The direct route from Troy to Ithaca

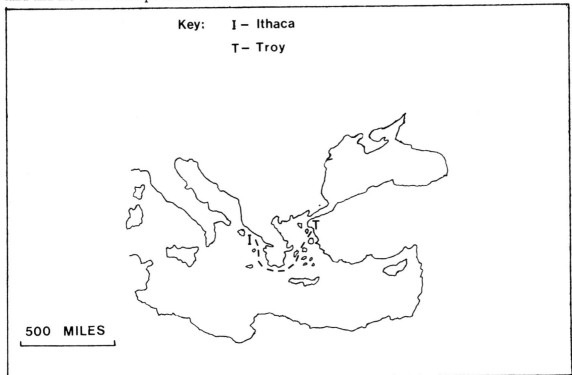

Key: I – Ithaca
        T – Troy

500 MILES

The journey home was not to be easy. He was to be driven off his course many times and have many great adventures and so take ten years to get home.

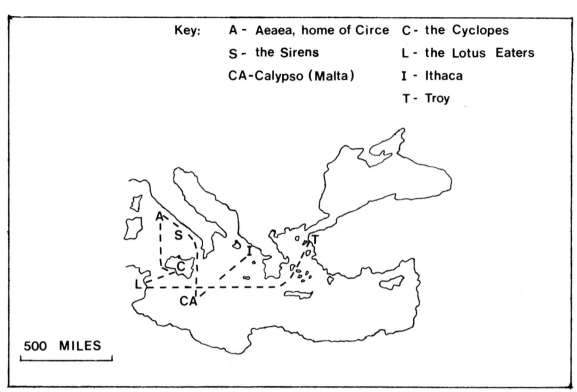

Key: A - Aeaea, home of Circe C - the Cyclopes
S - the Sirens L - the Lotus Eaters
CA - Calypso (Malta) I - Ithaca
T - Troy

500 MILES

The actual route home

Leaving Troy, Odysseus and his men headed for Ithaca but a violent storm drove them to North Africa, far past Ithaca, to the land of the 'Lotus Eaters', who were known by this name because they ate the lotus fruit. This produced such a pleasant feeling that anyone who ate it forgot about everything else. Some of Odysseus' men ate the fruit and they enjoyed it. They forgot all about the past and the future and wanted only to remain in the land of the Lotus Eaters. Odysseus, however, understood the situation and managed to drag the men back to the ships.

Odysseus and his men now sailed north to the island of Sicily which was inhabited by a tribe of huge giants called Cyclopes. These Cyclopes had each only one eye, set in the middle of the forehead above the nose. Their king was Polyphemus, who was the son of Poseidon, god of the sea. Odysseus and his men were hungry and by chance they wandered into the cave of Polyphemus. Polyphemus was not there and so Odysseus and his men helped themselves to some food and drink. Later Polyphemus returned and he became very angry when he saw some of his food and drink was gone. He devoured some of Odysseus' men to satisfy his own hunger and threatened to eat the others the following morning for

Odysseus' men eating the lotus fruit

breakfast. Polyphemus then brought the sheep he tended into his cave and closed the entrance with a big stone. The situation was desperate but Odysseus adopted a cunning plan. He made Polyphemus drunk with wine and the giant fell asleep. Then Odysseus sharpened a beam of wood and made its point burning hot. As some of his companions pulled back the one eyelid of Polyphemus Odysseus drove the beam solidly into the eye. Polyphemus sprang up and lunged at Odysseus. He could not catch him because he was now blind. Morning came and it was time for Polyphemus to let his sheep out to graze. Odysseus put the final part of his plan into operation. He and his men hid beneath the bellies of the sheep clinging on to the wool and, as Polyphemus stroked the backs of the sheep to make sure Odysseus did not escape that way, they succeeded

The blinding of Polyphemus

Circe turns Odysseus' men into pigs

in deceiving him. Odysseus now, however, had a very powerful enemy, the father of Polyphemus, Poseidon, who was angry with Odysseus for having blinded his son and was determined to do all he could to prevent Odysseus returning home to Ithaca.

After leaving Sicily Odysseus and his men were driven north towards Italy because of storms whipped up by Poseidon. In fact only the ship of Odysseus himself survived. Now this ship came to Aeaea, the island of Circe, who was a beautiful witch. She hated mankind and so when a scouting party sent by Odysseus came to her palace she entertained them very well and then turned them by her magic into pigs. One man, however, escaped and brought the news back to Odysseus. He set out to rescue his men and, on the way to the palace, was given a herb by Hermes, the messenger of the gods, that would guard him against Circe's magic. Protected by this and with sword in hand Odysseus threatened Circe so fiercely that she immediately turned his companions back into men and did no further damage. Circe, in fact, fell in love with Odysseus and he remained with her for a year but eventually the urge to return home came over him again.

Circe advised him to consult the ghost of the dead prophet, Teiresias. To do this Odysseus had to go down into the Land of the Dead. Circe helped him with her magic. Teiresias told Odysseus that he would indeed reach home safely as long as the cattle of Apollo were left unharmed. Odysseus left the Land of the Dead reassured.

Odysseus and his companions now sailed south down the coast of Italy until they came to the rocks of the Sirens. These Sirens had the bodies of birds but the faces of beautiful girls. They were lovely singers but were also very cruel. They distracted passing sailors with their singing to such an extent that the sailors forgot all about the steering of their ships, let the ships run into the rocks and were drowned. Odysseus had been warned about the Sirens by Circe and so, showing his usual cunning, he thought out a plan which would allow him to hear the beautiful singing but at the same time would get him past in safety. He plugged the ears of his men with wax and, with his own ears free, had his men tie him to the mast of the ship. He also instructed his men to disregard whatever he might do while passing and simply go on with their work. The plan was successful. Odysseus passed in safety and the Sirens, now that they had been defeated, jumped into the sea and turned into rocks.

After this Odysseus and his companions arrived at Thrinacia where the cattle of Apollo were. Odysseus warned his men that they should under no circumstances harm the cattle. There was, however, a tremendous shortage of food and the men became so hungry that one night, while Odysseus slept, they killed some of the cattle and had a feast. When Odysseus awoke he was horrified and set sail at once. Apollo, however, complained to Zeus and he brought on a mighty storm which destroyed the ship and killed all except Odysseus himself.

Odysseus, now the sole survivor, made a simple raft and eventually reached the island of Calypso, another beautiful witch. She fell in love with Odysseus and kept him there for seven years. He still remained homesick, however, and so Zeus ordered that he should be allowed to leave. After further adventures Odysseus arrived home in Ithaca, having been away twenty long years.

All was not well in Ithaca. The people had assumed that Odysseus was dead and so a group of suitors had descended upon the royal palace. Each suitor hoped to marry Odysseus' wife Penelope and so become king of Ithaca in his place. These suitors were very greedy and were living on the food and drink found in the palace. Odysseus, when he realized what was happening, decided that they should be taught a lesson. He made himself known to his son Telemachus. Penelope at this time announced that she would marry the man who could bend the great bow that Odysseus had left in the palace. The suitors all tried but failed. Then Odysseus himself, disguised as a

Sirens surround the ship

The great storm

beggar, came forward, bent the great bow and shot arrows at the suitors with it. Odysseus killed the suitors, helped by Telemachus, and now at long last was reunited with his faithful wife.

Things to do

Section A

1 Write the answers to the following questions in sentences:
   (a) Of which island was Odysseus king?
   (b) How long had Odysseus fought at Troy?
       On which side did he fight?
   (c) Give the names of Odysseus' wife and son.
2 Write out the following passage, filling in the blanks:
Leaving Troy Odysseus and his men were driven to North Africa to the land of the . . . . , who ate the lotus fruit. Some of Odysseus' men ate this fruit and forgot all about the past and the . . . . . . and wanted only to stay in the land of the . . . . . . However, ... dragged his men back to the ships.

Odysseus and his men now sailed north to the island of . . . . which was inhabited by a tribe of giants called . . . . The king of these giants was . . . . , son of . . . . Odysseus blinded . . . . and so had . . . . as a terrible enemy from now on.

Odysseus was then driven north towards Italy to the island of . . . . , a beautiful witch. She turned his men into . . . . . . but, under pressure, later changed them back to men.

Odysseus now sailed south to the rocks of the . . . . who were beautiful singers, but were also cruel and tried to kill passing sailors. Odysseus passed them and so they jumped into the sea and themselves became . . . . . .

Section B

1 Describe the scene in the palace on Ithaca when Odysseus and Telemachus killed the suitors.
2 Invent another adventure for Odysseus on his way home.
3 We know of the adventures of Odysseus because the Greek poet Homer wrote about them in the Odyssey. Homer wrote another poem about the siege and capture of Troy. What was it called?
4 Draw your favourite adventure of Odysseus.

2 In Search of the Golden Fleece

Jason was born in the city of Iolcus in Greece. His father was Aeson, the rightful king of the city, but Aeson's half-brother Pelias, wanting the throne, imprisoned Aeson and threatened to kill the infant Jason. To save his life, Jason was brought out of the city and looked after by the Centaur Cheiron, a man with the body of a horse.

The route to Colchis

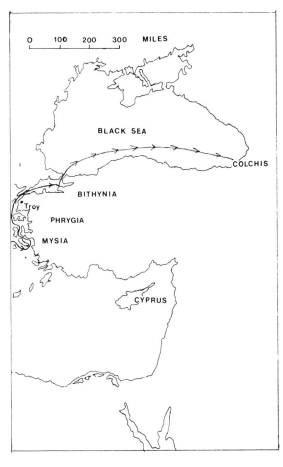

Jason and the Centaur Cheiron

Jason with one sandal

When Jason grew up, he decided to return to Iolcus to claim the throne. On the way he met an old woman who was afraid to cross a broad river by herself. Jason was glad to help and he picked her up on his back and carried her across. Suddenly she changed into a goddess and declared, 'I am Hera and, since you have helped me, I promise to help you from now on'. Jason felt reassured now for he had the queen of the gods and goddesses on his side.

Jason had lost a sandal in the river and so he arrived in Iolcus with one bare foot. Pelias, when he saw this, was immediately on his guard for an oracle had told him he would be killed by his own relations and had also warned him of a man with one bare foot.

Jason asked for the kingdom back. Pelias, in a panic, was determined to do all he could to get rid of him. He declared, 'There is only one way, Jason, in which you will get the kingdom back, and that is by searching for and bringing back to me the Golden Fleece from Colchis, a city on the Black Sea.' He said that this fleece would be a great treasure because it could cure illness and even restore life. Jason, confident of Hera's help, took up the challenge.

To go on this great voyage, Jason first of all needed a ship. He summoned Argus, a famous craftsman, and told him the story. He asked him to build a very fast ship, promising him great fame if he did so. Argus agreed to build it and also to go as one of the crew. With the help of Athena, the goddess of wisdom and crafts, he built a wonderful ship which could even sail without a helmsman. It was called the Argo, after the builder. Jason now needed a crew. He sent messengers all over Greece inviting many daring young men to join him. There flocked to Iolcus some of the greatest heroes who ever lived—Hercules, famous for his twelve fantastic labours, Castor and Pollux, the twin sons of Zeus, Peleus the father of the mighty Achilles, the wonderful minstrel Orpheus and Theseus, the killer of the Minotaur. In all there were fifty Argonauts, as the sailors were called, including Jason and Argus.

All was now ready and the Argonauts set sail. First of all they came to the island of Lemnos and were surprised to find it was inhabited only by women. These women, who had killed their husbands because of some insults, welcomed the Argonauts gladly and entertained them very well. The Argonauts, in fact, were tempted to stay there permanently with the women but Hercules reminded them of their mission and they dragged themselves away.

Later on the Argonauts ran short of water and so they put in to land at Mysia. The young Hylas, a great friend of Hercules,

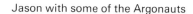
Jason with some of the Argonauts

Hylas

was sent to fetch some water at a spring. The nymphs of the spring, however, were attracted to the handsome youth and pulled him into the spring to be with them forever. Hercules stayed behind in Mysia to look for his friend and the Argonauts went on without him.

Next they came to Bithynia where Amycus was king. He was a famous boxer and challenged all strangers to fight. The young Pollux, one of the twins, accepted and, being faster on his feet, defeated the king and killed him.

The Argonauts were now about to enter the Black Sea. They had to go through the narrow Bosporus strait with great rocks at either side. Suddenly, as the Argonauts looked, these rocks clashed together, leaving no path for a ship. The Argonauts were amazed and frightened and wanted to return home, for they thought they had no hope of getting through, but Jason told them that these were the famous clashing rocks about which Phineus (a prophet) had warned him and advised him to seek omens from the gods. Jason had a dove with him and he let it go, as Phineus had instructed. 'If this dove comes back here safely' declared Jason, 'then that is a good sign.' The dove flew between the rocks losing only her tail feather and returned safely to Jason. He gave the order to go on and so, with the Argonauts rowing as hard as possible, the Argo sped

Pollux and Amycus

The Argo sails through the clashing rocks

between the rocks. The rocks did clash together but they damaged the Argo only slightly in the stern, just as the dove had lost her tail feather. From then on they remained motionless.

The Argonauts now sailed to the far end of the Black Sea to Colchis, where a savage dragon that never slept guarded the Golden Fleece in a wood. Jason visited Aeetes, the king of Colchis and owner of the Fleece, without delay and declared boldly, 'I want the Golden Fleece'. Aeetes replied, 'You may have it, only by performing certain tasks. First of all, you must yoke together two fire breathing bulls to a plough. Then you must plough a field sacred to Ares, god of war, and sow it with dragon's teeth. Immediately armed men will spring from these teeth. You have to kill them all. If you do this, there is still one further task. You must get past the ever watchful dragon that guards the Fleece.' These tasks seemed impossible to Jason but he agreed to attempt them the following day, for he desperately wanted the Fleece.

Jason, however, was about to receive some help. When he had been at the palace, Medea, Aeetes' daughter, had seen him and had been greatly attracted to him. She now went to see Jason at night and, being skilled in magic, offered him an ointment. She said, 'This will protect your body from all wounds, Jason. There is only one condition, you must take me back to Greece with you and marry me.' Jason agreed and he awaited the following day with greater confidence.

Next day the contest began. To everyone's surprise, Jason, protected by the ointment, yoked the bulls and ploughed the field, sowing the teeth. Armed men sprang up and prepared to attack Jason. However, he threw a boulder among them which made them fight and kill one another. The rest of them were killed by Jason. Aeetes was astonished by all this and then realized that Medea had helped Jason. He told her, 'If Jason gets past the dragon to the Fleece, you will die.' Medea said nothing but already she was planning ahead. During the night she left the palace, taking her little brother Absyrtus. She roused Jason, told him of her father's threat, and urged him to fetch the Fleece at once. Jason and Medea went through the wood where the Fleece was and suddenly they saw it, glowing in the distance. The dragon noticed them, however, and prepared to attack but Jason threw magic herbs, given him by Medea, into its eyes, which made it fall sleep.

Jason quickly gathered up the Fleece, roused the Argonauts from sleep, and set sail before dawn. Soon Aeetes realized what had happened and he pursued the Argo in his swiftest ship. When Medea saw her father catching up, she killed her brother Absyrtus and cut up his body into parts and threw them overboard. Aeetes recognized the remains of his son and stopped to pick them up. As he was being delayed in this way, the Argonauts escaped.

On the way home the Argo approached the island of Crete. Crete was defended by a brass giant called Talus. He had only one vein in his body, through which flowed a liquid called ichor. This ichor, which also flowed in the veins of the gods and kept them immortal, had been poured into Talus' body through a hole in his heel, which had then been filled by a nail.

Jason and Medea

Talus threatened the Argo but Medea came to the rescue again and offered him a drink which, in fact, was a sleeping potion. As the giant was dozing off, Poeas, an Argonaut especially skilled in archery, fired an arrow at the nail and knocked it out so that the ichor flowed out of Talus' body. He was helpless to stop this and thundered to the ground with a tremendous thud.

When they reached Greece the Argonauts disbanded. Jason and Medea took the Fleece to Pelias and demanded the kingdom back. They soon discovered however that terrible deeds had been done. Pelias had forced Jason's father Aeson to commit suicide and Jason's mother had died of a broken heart. Medea plotted revenge on Pelias. She told his daughters to cut up an old ram into bits and put them in boiling water. She then uttered a charm and a young lamb sprang from the water. In this way Medea convinced the daughters that she could make the old young again and, therefore, could make their father a

Jason collects the Golden Fleece
right: The daughters of Palias;
below: the death of Talus

young man again. They went through the same procedure with Pelias. His daughters cut him up into bits and put them in boiling water. They looked to Medea to utter her charm but she had vanished. Only then did the daughters realize they had been tricked into murdering their own father. Jason was avenged.

Jason, however, did not get the kingdom back, for Acastus, Pelias' son, banished both him and Medea from Iolcus and they fled to Corinth. Jason and Medea had a happy marriage for some years until Jason left Medea for Creusa, the daughter of the king of Corinth. Medea naturally was upset and she sent Creusa a wedding dress which, as soon as she put it on, went up in flames and burned her to death. Medea then killed the children from her marriage to Jason hoping to make Jason miserable for the rest of his life, and she fled to Athens. Eventually she became a Goddess. Jason, as Medea hoped, spent the rest of his life in misery and is said either to have committed suicide or to have died when the prow of the Argo fell on his head. However, he will always be remembered for his splendid courage in the quest for the Golden Fleece.

Things to do

Section A

1 Copy the following passage into your jotter, completing the blanks:
   Jason was born in the city of . . . . but as an infant was brought up by the Centaur . . . . to escape the cruelty of his wicked uncle . . . . , who had already imprisoned his father . . . . When Jason grew up, he wanted to return to . . . . and on the way he helped the goddess . . . . , who became his ally from then on. When Jason reached . . . . , his uncle . . . . said he could have the kingdom back provided he brought the . . . . from . . . . , a city on the . . . . Sea.
2 Write the answers to the following questions in your jotter. Answer in sentences.
   (a) Who built the Argo?
   (b) Name as many Argonauts as you can.
   (c) Which island was inhabited only by women?
   (d) Name the youth who was pulled into the spring by nymphs.

(e) In Bithynia there was a boxing match. Name the fighters and who won?

(f) What was the name of the strait that led into the Black Sea?

(g) Who was the king of Colchis?

(h) Name this king's daughter.

(i) Who was Absyrtus and how did he die?

(j) Who was the brass giant who lived on Crete and what was the name of the liquid that flowed through him?

(k) How did Pelias die? Write an answer of two to three sentences.

3 Copy the following crossword into your notebook and then try to solve it. It deals with the Jason story.

Clues

Across

3 The wicked uncle
4 Queen of the gods and goddesses
6 Island inhabited by women
9 He killed the Minotaur
10 He performed many labours
12 The land where the Fleece was

Down

1 The boat-builder
2 He was dragged into a spring
3 One of the twins
5 King of Colchis
7 The minstrel among the Argonauts
8 They started from here
11 The Centaur

Section B

1 A sign of the zodiac is called after two of the Argonauts. Which two and which sign? Make a list of the other signs of the zodiac.
2 Talus could be damaged in the heel. Who else was able to be hurt only in this area?
3 Imagine you are Jason as an old man. Look back over the voyage to get the Fleece and write a paragraph on what sticks out most in your memory.
4 Make a drawing of your favourite part of the story.
5 Make a model of the Argo. It has only one deck of oars and there are fifty of them.

3 Mission Impossible

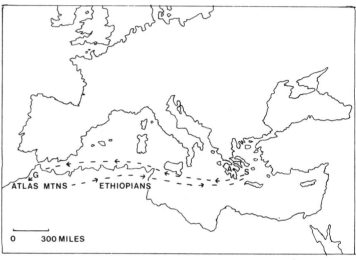

The flight of Perseus

A – Argos
S– Seriphos
G– where the Gorgons lived,
 in the farthest west.

Acrisius was the king of Argos. He longed for a son to succeed him but unfortunately all he had was a daughter called Danae. He decided to consult the oracle at Delphi about whether he would have a son and was told, 'You will never have a son but you will have a grandson and he will kill you.' Acrisius naturally did not want his daughter to have any children and so he shut her up in a dungeon which was guarded by watchdogs. Zeus, however, found a way in and she gave birth to a boy called Perseus. Acrisius found it impossible to kill his grandson with his own hand but he enclosed both the child and his mother in a chest and threw it into the sea, hoping they would be drowned. The chest, however, was driven on to the island of Seriphos in the Aegean Sea and was caught by a fisherman called Dictys. He opened it up, found Danae and Perseus inside, and brought

Dictys finding the chest

them to his brother Polydectes, the king of the island. Polydectes was very kind and treated them well.

When Perseus grew up, Polydectes wanted to marry Danae but she refused. He was very upset at this and became violent, wanting to kill Danae. He was prevented, however, by fear of Perseus and so he planned to get him out of the way. He said he was going to marry another woman and arranged the wedding, asking for a horse from each of the guests. Perseus was among the guests but, being poor, he could not give a horse. Polydectes hoped Perseus would be embarrassed because of this and would make some rash statement about what he would give. Perseus *was* embarrassed and declared he would give as a present the head of the Gorgon Medusa.

There were, in fact, three Gorgons and Medusa was the only one who could be killed. They were horribly ugly sisters who had snakes instead of hair, wings and huge claws on their hands. Medusa was so ugly that any person who looked at her face immediately was turned to stone, and, as was discovered later, the face had the very same effect even after she had been killed.

Medusa

Polydectes, when he heard Perseus' offer, immediately accepted, for this would get Perseus out of the way and give him the chance to kill Danae. The gods took pity on Perseus and provided him with some armour. Hades lent him his helmet which would make him invisible. Athena gave him a bright shield so that he could look at Medusa's reflection and see what she was doing without actually looking at her, and Hermes gave him winged sandals, to enable him to fly, and a very sharp sword.

Perseus now set out to find the Gorgons. At last he flew above them and he looked closely at them by means of his shield, for they were asleep. He remembered not to look directly. He stared at their ugliness for some time, then came down to the earth and approached Medusa, again using the bright shield. He struck her once with his sword and that was enough. He placed the head in a bag, making sure he did not look, leapt into the air and made his escape.

On the way back to Seriphos, Perseus paid a visit to Atlas, the giant who held up the heavens on his shoulders. He was very unfriendly and so Perseus showed him the head of Medusa, which turned him into a mountain range. These are the Atlas Mountains in Africa.

Perseus continued his journey and flew over the land of the Ethiopians whose king was Cepheus. He looked down and saw chained to a rock a very beautiful girl.

He fell in love with her immediately, swept down to the earth and asked the girl to tell him how she came to be in that position. The girl whose name was Andromeda, told him that her mother Cassiope had boasted that she (the mother) was even more beautiful than the Nereids, who were sea-goddesses. Poseidon, god of the sea, apparently had resented this boast and sent a huge monster to destroy the country. Andromeda's father, King Cepheus, consulted an oracle and was told that, if he wanted to get rid of the monster, he must sacrifice his daughter to it. She was now waiting for the monster to appear. Although she had been promised in marriage to her uncle Phineus, he had not as yet tried to rescue her. Just at this point Andromeda's parents appeared, lamenting the fate of their daughter. The monster also appeared from the sea, making a great roar. Perseus took immediate action. He declared to the parents that he would kill the monster and save Andromeda if they would give her to him in marriage. They agreed, forgetting she was already betrothed. Perseus soared up into the air and, striking the monster fiercely many times with his sword, killed it. Andromeda was released and, since she had fallen in love with Perseus, the wedding was held shortly afterwards.

Perseus and Andromeda

Perseus swooping down on the monster

During the wedding feast Phineus arrived with some armed men, demanding Andromeda back. Cepheus now showed his true colours. He had not really wanted Andromeda to marry Perseus and now supported Phineus' cause. Perseus was trapped, for the armed men kept rushing into the hall. He killed a few of them but sheer weight of numbers was overcoming him. He resorted to his ultimate weapon, the Gorgon's head, which turned 200 men into stone. Phineus himself, who had hidden behind an altar during the fighting, was among these and the statue of him was an everlasting testimony of his cowardice. It showed him pleading for his life from Perseus. Even his cowardly tears could be seen in the marble.

Perseus now took Andromeda back to Seriphos. He found that his mother Danae and Dictys, the fisherman who had discovered them in the chest, were in Athena's temple, trying

Perseus about to kill Acrisius with the discus

to escape from King Polydectes, who still wanted to kill them. Perseus solved their problem once and for all by showing the king the head of Medusa and turning him to stone.

Perseus now longed to return to his native Argos. Acrisius, his grandfather, heard that he was coming and, to avoid the fulfilment of the prophecy that he would be killed by his grandson, fled to the town of Larissa. Perseus stopped off there on his way to Argos to take part in some games. He was competing in the discus but the wind took his discus off its course and it killed a spectator. This was Acrisius. The prophecy had come true.

Perseus discovered that this spectator was his grandfather. He was greatly depressed by the killing and refused to become king of Argos for the place reminded him of the unfortunate event. Instead, he founded a new city which became very famous—Mycenae.

Things to do

Section A

1 Write out the following passage, filling in the blanks:

. . . . , the king of Argos, longed for a son but had only a daughter called . . . . . . He consulted the oracle at . . . . . . and was told he would be killed by his . . . . . . He, therefore, did not wish his daughter . . . . . . to have children but . . . . . . reached the daughter and she produced a boy called . . . . . . The king then put his daughter and her son into a . . . . . . and threw it into the sea. This, however, was found by a fisherman called . . . . . . and he brought the daughter and her child to king . . . . . .

2 Write the heading *Perseus and Andromeda*, then answer the following questions in sentences:

(a) What did king Polydectes want from each guest as a wedding present and what did Perseus offer?

(b) What did the gods and goddesses give Perseus to protect himself?

(c) What did Perseus do to Atlas?

(d) What was the name of the girl chained to the rock?

(e) How had she come to be chained there?

(f) To whom was the girl promised in marriage? Was there anything unusual about this proposed match?

(g) In the battle in the hall, how many men were turned to stone?

(h) What was the final fate of King Polydectes?

(i) How was Perseus' grandfather killed?

(j) What great town was founded by Perseus?

3 Give a description of the Gorgon Medusa.

Section B

1 You are Perseus. You have just killed a man at the games at Larissa. Describe the accident and then your feelings when you learn of the prophecy and the identity of the man you have killed.

2 Tell, by means of small pictures, how Perseus won Andromeda. You could add conversation to the pictures. Here is an example:

Four other pictures could complete the story—Andromeda telling Perseus what had happened, Perseus declaring to Andromeda's parents that he will save her if they allow him to marry her, Perseus killing the monster, and finally Perseus turning the men to stone in the hall.

3 Draw a picture of the head of Medusa or of Andromeda chained to the rock or of the statue of Phineus.

4 Try to make a model of the head of Medusa.

4 A Strong Man Triumphs

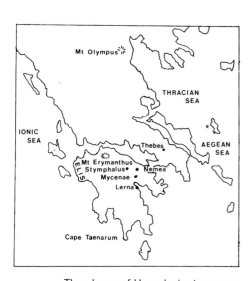

The places of Hercules' adventures

Hercules, whom the Greeks called Heracles, was the son of Zeus and a mortal called Alcmene. She later married Amphitryon, a famous Theban general, and Hercules was brought up as their son.

Hera, wife of Zeus, was always jealous of Hercules because he was not her son and even before he was eight months old she sent two snakes into his cradle to devour him. She had not, however, realized the immense strength and courage of Hercules even at this early stage and he strangled the snakes.

Hercules as a child

Hercules spent his childhood and youth learning all he could. He was taught how to fight, shoot with a bow and arrows, drive a chariot, play the lyre and sing, and eventually became the pupil of the Centaur Cheiron, under whom he brought his skills to perfection. Cheiron had taught Jason also and indeed one of the first exploits of Hercules was to go with the Argonauts to get the Golden Fleece. He did not remain with them, however, for he left to look for his lost friend Hylas.

On his return home to Thebes, Hercules married Princess Megara and in effect ruled Thebes. Hera, however, still plagued him and one day she afflicted him with such a fit of madness that he murdered his wife and children. Hercules, when he recovered his sanity, vowed to make up for this crime and he consulted the oracle at Delphi. The oracle commanded him to go to Eurystheus, king of Mycenae, and do whatever he ordered. Hercules went to Mycenae and was given twelve great tasks to perform, known now as the Labours of Hercules. His only companion during the labours was to be Iolaus, the eldest son of his half brother, Iphicles. The gods did not desert him completely, for, before he undertook the labours, he was armed by them. From Athena he received a coat of arms and helmet, from Hermes a sword, from Poseidon a horse, from Zeus a shield, a bow and arrows from Apollo, and from Hephaestus a golden cuirass and bronze boots. Hercules' favourite weapon, however, was a massive club which was made of wood and which he himself had cut.

Hercules and the Nemean lion

The first labour was to kill the Nemean lion, which was destroying the country near Mycenae. Hercules boldly attacked the lion with his club, pursued him to his lair and choked him to death. He then carried the dead beast to Mycenae on his shoulders, skinned it and from then on wore the skin as a garment with its head and teeth as a protection for his own head. Eurystheus was so astonished by the courage of Hercules that he ordered him never again to enter Mycenae when he returned from his labours but to remain outside.

The second labour was to kill the Hydra of Lerna. This was a terrible monster. It had nine snake heads, one of which could not be killed. When Hercules cut off one of the heads, two more would grow in its place. To prevent this, Iolaus burned the neck with a hot iron. Then Hercules cut off the immortal head and buried it under a great rock. He dipped his arrows in the blood of the Hydra, which made them poisonous.

Hercules and the Hydra

For his third labour Hercules was ordered to bring back to Eurystheus a stag, called the Ceryneian Hind, which was famous for its incredible speed, golden horns and bronze hooves. Hercules pursued the animal for a whole year and at last caught it in a trap. He went as far as the land of the Hyperboreans in the far north of the world in his search. As he was returning to Eurytheus with the stag, Artemis, goddess of hunting, snatched it from him, and was angry with him because he had captured an animal that was sacred to her. Hercules explained why he had done it and she released the stag.

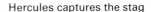

Hercules captures the stag

Hercules and the boar

Hercules' fourth labour was to capture alive a wild boar which was destroying the neighbourhood of Erymanthus in Western Greece. He pursued the boar closely, trapped it in some snow, bound it in chains and took it back to Eurystheus.

The fifth labour was to clean in one day the stables of Augeas, the king of Elis. Augeas had a huge number of oxen and goats and the stables where they were kept had never been cleaned. Hercules simply diverted the course of a neighbouring river through the stables and the force of the water was great enough to carry away all the dung and filth.

As his sixth labour Hercules had to kill the birds that flocked to lake Stymphalus in Arcadia and were destroying the country-side round about the lake. These birds had bronze beaks, bronze claws and bronze wings and they ate human beings. There were too many of them for Hercules to pick them off individually with his bow and arrows. What he did was to make

Above: Shooting the birds
Right: Diverting the river

a rattle and he created such a din with the rattle that the birds flew up into the air in a huge group, in an absolute panic. Hercules shot most of them while they did not realize what was happening.

The seventh labour was to capture a fierce, fire-breathing bull which was creating terror on the island of Crete. King Minos of Crete was prepared to give Hercules all the help he needed but, after a great struggle, he managed to subdue the beast himself. The bull was brought to Mycenae where it was dedicated by Eurystheus to Hera.

To capture the four savage horses of Diomedes, the king of Thrace, was the eighth labour. These horses lived on human flesh and they were usually given the bodies of guests of the king who were unaware of the fate that awaited them. Hercules killed Diomedes with his club, fed his body to the horses and, as soon as he had satisfied their hunger, overpowered them without too much trouble.

The ninth labour was to bring back to Eurytheus the belt of Hippolyte, the queen of the Amazons. The Amazons were a tribe of fierce women who managed their affairs and protected themselves without the aid of husbands. They lived in the city of Themiscyra in Asia Minor. When Hippolyte saw Hercules,

she was attracted to him and offered him her belt as a sign of her love. At that moment the other Amazons, without Hippolyte's knowledge, attacked Hercules because they thought he was planning to snatch their queen away. Hercules believed he had been tricked. He killed Hippolyte, took her belt off, and made his escape with it.

Hercules' tenth labour was to fetch the cattle of a monster called Geryon, who lived on an island in the far west. Geryon was exceedingly strong and had three heads and three bodies, joined together at the waist. Hercules had also to contend with a herdsman and a two-headed dog, called Orthos, who guarded the cattle. He killed both the dog and the herdsman with his club, and proceeded to kill Geryon very cunningly, by firing one arrow sideways through all three of his bodies. He was able now to take the cattle away.

The eleventh labour was to get the golden apples of the Hesperides, the daughters of Atlas. He was the giant who had been condemned to support the heavens on his shoulders and the Hesperides, along with Ladon, a dragon which never slept, were the guardians of these apples, which had been a wedding present from Hera to Zeus. Hercules looked for Nereus, a god of the sea, and forced him to tell how he could get the apples. Nereus advised him to try to persuade Atlas to fetch the apples. When Hercules found Atlas he said he would help but Hercules must first of all kill the dragon and support the heavens for him

Left: The Cretan bull; *above:* Hercules and Diomedes; *below:* Hercules and Hippolyte

Geryon

Hercules and Cerberus

while he was collecting the apples. Hercules agreed, killed Ladon with an arrow and took the weight of the heavens on his broad shoulders. Atlas, helped by his daughters, gathered three of the apples and brought them back to Hercules. Atlas, however, realized he was free of his burden and had no intention of taking it back. Hercules tricked Atlas by saying he was not very comfortable and that he wanted him to hold the heavens for a few moments while he put a pad on his head and shoulders. Atlas placed the apples on the ground and took his burden back. Hercules cheerfully picked the apples up and carried them to Eurystheus.

The twelfth and last labour was the most difficult. Hercules had to bring up from the Land of the Dead the three-headed dog Cerberus, who guarded its entrance. He went down to the Land of the Dead at Taenarum and eventually spoke to Hades. Hades allowed him to make the attempt on Cerberus, provided he used no weapons. Hercules again relied on his great strength and gripped the dog firmly by the throat. Cerberus put up a tremendous battle but finally gave in and Hercules pulled him up to the earth. Eurystheus, when he saw the dog, did not want him and ordered Hercules to take him back again to the Land of the Dead.

In this way Hercules performed his twelve labours to make up for the murder of his wife and children. He performed other fantastic deeds and became one of the gods on Mount Olympus.

Things to do

Section A

1 Write out the following passage in your notebook, completing the blanks.

Hercules was the son of . . . . . . and a mortal called . . . . . . and because of this, was hated by . . . . . . She hated him so much that, even while he was still a baby, she sent two . . . . . . into his cradle to devour him. Hercules survived this and later became a pupil of the Centaur . . . . . . under whom . . . . . . had also studied.

After his return from the voyage to get the . . . . . . Hercules married Princess . . . . . . but . . . . . . still hated him and made him so mad that he killed his family. To make up for this, he had to do whatever . . . . . . , the king of . . . . . . , ordered. He gave Hercules twelve great tasks, known as the . . . . . .

2 Write out a description of Hercules. Mention what he might be wearing and his weapons. You could add a drawing of him.

3 Below you are given a list of the twelve labours, all jumbled up. Write them out in your jotter, placing them in the correct order.

    to clean the stables of Augeas
    to fetch the horses of Diomedes
    to kill the Hydra
    to get the golden apples
    to capture the boar of Erymanthus
    to get Cerberus
    to kill the Nemean lion
    to capture the Cretan bull
    to fetch the belt of Hippolyte
    to kill the birds of Stymphalus
    to bring back the hind
    to fetch the cattle of Geryon

4 Choose the labour that interested you most and write a paragraph about it.

5 Draw a picture of another labour and write a sentence or two to explain what you have drawn.

Section B

1 Copy out the dots below in your jotter. They represent a creature Hercules met. Join them up and discover the creature.

2 Write a newspaper report on one of the labours. Make sure it is one you have not already tackled. Give the report a headline, make a drawing to illustrate it, and then add your on the spot report.

Acknowledgments

Thanks are due to The Society of Authors as the literary representative of the Estate of A. E. Housman and Jonathan Cape Ltd, publishers of A. E. Housman's *Collected Poems* for permission to quote lines from 'Look not in my eyes, for fear'; and to Penguin Books Ltd for permission to use an extract from Homer: *The Iliad*, translated by E. V. Rieu (Penguin Classics, 1950) pp. 12–14 and pp. 77–78.

The Publisher's thanks are also due to the following for permission to reproduce copyright photographs:
Kunsthistorisches Museum, Vienna: p. 2 (Leonard Beck: *St. George and the Dragon*); Hale Observatories, courtesy Royal Astronomical Society: p. 3 (top); Mansell Collection: cover, pp. 3 (bottom left), 11 (top right), 20, 29, 30 (right), 42 (bottom), 49 (both), 59 (left), 81, 82, 103 (bottom); University of Athens, Department of Geology and Palaeontology: p. 4; Phaidon Press, courtesy Cooper-Bridgeman Library: p. 6 (left); Metropolitan Museum of Art, Rogers Fund: p. 6 (right); Sonia Halliday Photographs: p. 7 (both); Popperfoto: pp. 9, 30 (left), 35 (top), 65, 83 (left); National Tourist Organization of Greece: pp. 11 (top left, top middle, and middle right), 42 (top); Marilynn Zipes: p. 21; P. Gallias: p. 31; Michael Holford Library: pp. 32 (top and middle, both Gerry Clyde), 33, 35 (left), 41 (right); Mexican National Tourist Council: p. 32 (bottom); Mary Evans Picture Library: pp. 35 (bottom right), K. Corsar: p. 36; Controller of Her Majesty's Stationery Office, Crown copyright, courtesy Department of the Environment: p. 41 (left); Robert Harding Associates: p. 59 (right); Photoresources/C. M. Dixon: pp. 64 (right), 83 (bottom right), 84.
The drawings on pp. 31, 33 (bottom) and 36 are by Philip Page.

116